WALT GRISCHUK

Supply Chain Brutalization

The Handbook for Contract Manufacturing

Copyright © 2009 Walt Grischuk
All rights reserved.

ISBN: 1-4392-6216-0
ISBN-13: 9781439262160

To order additional copies, please contact us.
BookSurge
www.booksurge.com
1-866-308-6235
orders@booksurge.com

Contents

Introduction	xiii
1. Bad News	1
2. What is a Contract Manufacturer?	11
Definitions / Types	11
Service Offerings	18
Shapes and Sizes	23
Markets Served	25
Technology	28
3. Industry Historical Overview	31
Origins and Trends	31
Growth into Market Segment	34
Mergers and Acquisitions	35
Globalization	41
CMs in Recession	42
4. Industry Market Overview	45
Low-cost Alternatives	45
Emerging Regions	46
ODM	51
ODM vs. OEM	53
What Sends it Away	55
What Brings it Back	58
Culture	62
Humanity	66
Environment	67
Economic Swings	71
Summation	77

5. Philosophical DNA — 79
- The Dilemma — 79
- Business Methodology — 85

6. Core Competence — 87
- Service / Contract Administration — 87
- Change Management — 92
- Manufacturing / Process Control / Planning — 93
- Materials / Inventory Control / Supply Chain Management — 98

7. Risk Management — 107

8. Quality Systems — 111

9. Competitiveness — 115

10. Financial models — 117
- Quote Equals Standard — 117
- Set the Standard — 119
- Monitor the Variance — 121
- P&L Reporting — 126
- Turn the Assets — 131

11. HBO — 137

12. Inside the OEM — 141
- Business Models — 142
- Core Competencies — 143
- Financial Models — 144
- HBO — 144

13. Reasons to outsource — 149
- Time to Market — 149
- Capacity — 150
- Technical — 150
- Financial — 150
- Core Competence — 151

14. Fundamentals / DDFM — 153
- DFM / DFT — 153
- Design Documentation for Manufacturing / DDFM — 155
- Part Numbering Schemes (White Paper) — 158
- Technical Specifications and Formats — 179
- Technical and Quality Requirements — 182
- Change Control — 183

15. Outsourcing Strategy / Selection — 187
- Objectives — 187
- Roles and Responsibilities — 187
- Scope of Work — 188
- Supplier Search — 189
- RFI — 192
- RFP — 194
- E-Bid — 195
- Benchmarking — 196
- Evaluation — 196
- Survey — 197
- Award — 199

16. Production Ramp — 203
- Alpha — 203
- Beta — 204
- Proto
- Pilot — 205
- Production — 206

17. Sustaining / SCE — 209
- Order Commitments — 209
- Change Management
- Cost Reductions — 211
- QBR — 212
- Disengagement — 213

18. Summary   **217**
    The New Order

TLA (Three Letter Acronyms)   **231**

Acknowledgements

Many thanks go out to my colleagues who have shared their thoughts and industry experiences over the past two decades.

This study was compiled over several years of working with clients and hearing their thoughts, challenges, and rants. We tried to answer some of them with white papers. The white papers turned into lectures—the lectures then expanded into chapters.

Special thanks to my friend and colleague, Dr. Brian Anthony of MIT, who provided the venue to vent and the encouragement to get it all down on paper. Also, to Jesse Ambrosina of J. Ambrosina Consulting, who provided validation of certain points of stress in the recurring confusion of reality over logic. Others just shared their stories, especially when the conversation swung over to how things really worked out there.

INTRODUCTION

Of the $1 trillion (US) plus manufacturing market, $300 billion is outsourced annually, into the waiting arms of the contract manufacturer. While CMs take on many shapes and sizes, the successful contract manufacturer realizes that they are actually in a service industry, generating their profits from efficiencies in manufacturing and business process execution while satisfying their customers. Metal forming, garment sewing, circuit board assembly, etc., all share the same need for tenacity in asset utilization and keeping a watchful eye on the expense line. And when run right, these companies can turn a very respectable profit.

The largest contract manufacturing sector is the Electronics Manufacturing Services (EMS) industry. This industry (as well as most of the others) feeds off of the electronics industry, which, with the help of the consumer electronics boom, creates most of the trillion dollars worth of product each year. It is this manufacturing sector and market space from which this study derives much of its information, as it dominates the outsourcing economy.

Whether you are an Original Equipment Manufacturer (OEM) looking to subcontract product manufacturing or an entrepreneur looking to invest in a manufacturing company, an inside look of how this industry operates will show some real life differences between *World Class* manufacturing's *Best Practices,* and the actual behavior that drives their bottom lines.

The case will be made that many OEMs do not effectively manage their new product development and demand management. And even the largest of CMs can be challenged when introducing new products into production or reacting to customers' ongoing scheduling needs. It is the low and fixed cost that drew the OEM to the CM, yet they do not understand why they are not serviced in the way they were told they would be.

Yes, there are those companies that can manage both, and some that do it well. But, many are bottom line driven—especially the publicly held companies. And when the end of the month, quarter, or year rolls around, the rules, if any, are abandoned. Sales are maximized and inventory is minimized in a flurry of schedule "pull-ins" and "push-outs."

Reacting to, and managing the OEM's needs while protecting their own bottom line is the way of life at a CM. The CM in turn manages its supply chain in the same way, passing on the pain.

So why don't you do hear or read about this? It's simple: how would it sound if a VP of supply chain at a $10 billion OEM boasted about putting the brakes on $30 million of inbound product from their contract manufacturers in the last week of the year, in order to posture their inventory position—without regard for any purchase order or contract that might be in place (true story). "*Negotiating* the schedule change was easy . . ." Not exactly the kind of thing you will read about in *Purchasing Magazine* or *EBN* (*Electronics Business News*).

This behavior in business relationships happens every day, on every level. While we all rally around "best practices" and "lean" manufacturing, these trendy buzz words tend to get left on the conference room grease board while the CM's materials group is trying to figure out why the production lines keep going down because of inventory inaccuracies. And over at the OEM, a new products team is launching yet another disaster well inside of lead time.

Peeling back the onion in a "root cause" analysis at both the CM and the OEM, reveal the common flaw: people. In addition to the fact that a human resource is a variable (some perform better than others), the fact is, some have their own agenda—one that may differ from the company's mission. It may be the company itself that put the specific goals and objectives on the individual that drives this behavior. Also, a personal agenda with an empire-building mentality may drive behavior in the wrong direction. Human Behavior in Organizations (HBO) has more of an impact on the performance of companies than you might think.

This study will first provide the reader with a flyover of the contract manufacturing industry, reviewing the various styles and types of companies that reside within it. We will then look closer at business processes, financial performance, and of course, behavior. The examples presented are true happenings in the industry. For some, we will not name the companies, out of professional courtesy. Finally, we will look at how it's all done, taking the reader through the sequential steps of outsourcing, including the dynamics of managing third party manufacturing.

The knowledge taken away will provide insight on how these businesses perform and behave. For those who will embark on an outsourcing mission, we will scope out the lay of the land and the ground rules for an OEM/CM relationship. Also, the critical elements to successfully award, launch, and manage outsourced production at a third party facility will be explained in a how to and how not to manner, demonstrating the impact of critical path decisions.

Living in this manic industry has proved educational indeed. The contributors to this study have spent many years and held a variety of roles in numerous manufacturing companies of varying sizes over the last 20 years of this industry's evolution. Where this industry takes us next is not clear. But, as the increasing "need" for consumer goods and electronics continues and new, low-cost economic zones emerge, competition will remain fierce. This will only lower the margins and thin the operating budgets of today's already "lean" (no pun intended) manufacturing enterprises.

Will something give in the industry to cause a monumental change in the way business is done? Doubtful. For as long as there is growing capacity (supply) to satisfy market demand, nature will take its course. Even with a great new philosophy, the bottom line approach to business—at both the CM and OEM—will forsake any real initiative to be creative and supportive to the supply chain's "value partners." Even after tanking together in 2001, the rebuilding, for the most part, was with thicker walls to insulate them from each other's misfortunes—in readiness for the next downturn, which is now upon us.

1. Bad News

Dear (your name,)

We regret to inform you that your uncle has passed away. He died a childless widower, and had amended his will after his wife passed last spring.

His estate is to be divided between you and your brother, Larry, as you both brought him happiness throughout the years.

To you, he left his company, Megatron Inc., the company that made him very rich. Megatron is a contract manufacturing company which consists of four facilities. Three facilities are within 20 miles of each other, the fourth is in Tijuana, Mexico.

The good news is Megatron has $15-20 million in revenue annually and there is no evidence of any customers leaving or canceling any programs. In fact, there is growth, even in this down economy.

The bad news: the COO and CFO have just resigned.

More bad news: the company is burning cash at a rate of $100K per month (after the two overpaid execs exited). There is about $500K left in the bank and they have shut down your line of credit, leaving you an OOC (Out of Cash) date of five months.

Enclosed you will find reports from your accountant for each facility, along with all the keys. Good luck!

Facility One:

Sheet Metal Fabrication

10,000 sq ft
20 people
$2 million revenue
15% net profit

Significant cost drivers:
$5000/mo. rent
$75K/yr. salesperson
7 staff (O/H) (avg. $52K/yr. ea.)
13 DL (Direct labor force) (avg. $24K/yr. ea.)
Increasing raw material costs (eroded 10% of profits from the previous year)
Bid rate: $28/hr. (competitive)

Business overview:
This is the baby that started it all for your uncle. An Instant positive cash flow was achieved when his customer, AlarmCo consigned the material and Megatron punched out control panels for $1 each. Each panel then created 50 cents of scrap metal that was sold at the end of each month.

After making over a million of these units, AlarmCo sourced the panels in India using injection mold plastics. Megatron still sees other business from them, but the most of this division's revenue is spread out over 4 steady, long term customers.

Sales have been flat over the last three years with only one new customer partially offsetting the above migration offshore. Your salesperson advises that raising prices to recoup the material cost increases will result in losing business to the hungry competition.

Facility Two:

Cable Assembly

15,000 sq ft
15 people
$1.5 million in revenue
Break even

Significant cost drivers:
$100K/yr salesman
4 staff (avg. $52K yr. ea.)
11 DL (avg. $24K yr. ea.)
No rent. Facility resides in a small 4-unit strip mall, which you own. The other three tenants cover the overhead, each paying $2500 per month.
Bid Rate: $35/hr. (competitive)

Business overview:
Your uncle's buddy was his tenant in the strip mall. Like most manufacturers, his little cable assembly shop did business with AlarmCo. He told your uncle it was profitable, but three years ago it was time to retire, and he offered it to your uncle for a fair price.

Business seems to plod along, and the salesperson is really the one running the show. The rest of the staff looks to him for guidance, as the previous owner was also the general manager and your uncle didn't pay much attention to it after he bought it.

For the past two years, about half of your revenue came from AlarmCo, supporting their custom install team that needs a 2 week turn on delivery (and can't source these cables in China). The rest has been short run, quick turn requirements from many customers. It seems these jobs are dragging the shop down, as the production from

4

AlarmCo is quoted with a 40% gross profit and all costs appear to be in line.

The salesperson advises that they have to earn their way with the new customers and the short run/ not so profitable jobs are the future.

Facility Three:

EMS: PCB assembly

40,000 sq ft
60 people
$10-15 million revenue
10-15% loss

Significant cost drivers:
$5K/mo. mortgage
$100K/yr. salesperson
20 staff (avg. $52K/yr. ea.)
40 DL (avg-$24K yr. ea.)
Bid rate: $45/hr. (competitive)

Business overview:
Your uncle inherited the property and the conversion from a warehouse to EMS company was done via equity loan when AlarmCo asked him if he would assemble PCB's. He got filthy rich on this business, because—back then—he was the only source in the region. The job started as consignment, where AlarmCo delivered kits of material, then, over time, migrated to turnkey.

The new versions of these systems are now made in China, but there is a considerable amount of the old models sold each year under a maintenance and repair contract. Your uncle was smart and made "end of life" purchases, stockpiling unique components so he could never lose the business. The revenue on this is about $2 million a year, but it loses about $250K, due to the increase of manufacturing costs over the years.

Your uncle did not raise prices because there were/are new opportunities at AlarmCo on some special alarms for the FAA and Navy, which could not be outsourced internationally. Presently, this new business is another $5 million a year in surface mount PCB work from AlarmCo—operating at break even due to some start up issues and aggressive bidding due to new competition in the area. But the first builds were successful and the business is ramping and should hit $10 million and net about 10% profit next year (your agreed to cost model with the customer provides 14% gross margin). The program manager reports the relationship is solid and they will receive more quotes for other products soon.

There is also other new business coming in. Your salesperson reports two new customers have just launched a total of 20 new assemblies. The revenue is promising; perhaps a $3–5 million increase, and 20 more are in development. But the minimum purchases on the many line items of materials have killed your inventory turns (and cash flow). The suppliers are getting nervous, as you have everyone pushed out at 60 days…or more.

BTW-
You are also sitting on $3 million in pure excess material, not including the legacy product end of life buys. Over half of this was created to ramp the new programs.

Facility Four:

EMS
Tijuana, Mexico- light assembly, cable assemblies, limited manual PCB assembly

25,000 sq feet
30 people
$750K in revenue
10% loss

Significant cost drivers:
5 Staff (avg. $24K/yr. ea.)
25 DL (avg. $3K/yr. ea.)
Rent: $2500 /mo.
Freight: $2000/ mo.
No sales staff
13 weeks severance paid by company if let go
Bid Rate- $8/hr (competitive)

Business overview:
Your uncle wanted to dive into the low-cost Mexico scenario but never committed the time and resources needed to make a go of it, as he was spending too much time on his new yacht—which, by the way, he bequeathed to your brother Larry (along with a trust fund to maintain it, fuel it, and keep the crew).

The costs to run the facility are more than the wages, with a large freight bill for the trucking logistics. This is due to the needs of the only significant customer, who is located in San Diego. The customer is in the day planner business and the assembly of the planners is done at the Tijuana facility in a consignment fashion. The freight was negotiated into the deal and has resulted in a continuous shuttle back and forth delivering planners and picking up more kits.

There are a couple of cable projects and a PCB project, but these are offloads from a nearby manufacturer and they come and go as needed, totaling about $50K in consignment revenue.

There you have it.

The clock is ticking and you only have a few precious months before you run out of cash and cannot pay the suppliers to keep the production lines fed. And Larry has made it clear that you are not invited on his two year, around the world cruise.

If your mind is racing about the cash-out value of the real estate and assets, then close this book and transfer to Capital Venture 101.

This is about manufacturing. The sheet metal shop, as it sits, puts $300K in your pocket. And there is much more money to be made, if you can survive the next 6 to 12 months and get things right side up.

So, if you would like to go for it, read this study about contract manufacturing companies, customers, and people that reside in both. The fact that you now have some skin in the game will make some of the points of this book stand out. When you finish, come back here and make your moves.

You will have many options to cut costs and raise income. Some can be done quickly, extending your OOC date, while others will take time, but are needed for long term viability.

Remember, your staff is already thin, the economy is in the toilet, and your competitors are standing right behind you waiting for any opportunity to steal your business. And, losing a significant customer will take you down—so tread lightly…

Not pretty? This is life in contract manufacturing—and you're in it!

2. What is a Contract Manufacturer?

Definitions / Types

A *contract manufacturer* (CM) is an enterprise, company, concern, or individual that provides a manufacturing <u>service</u> to another company. This can be at the component level, such as a machined piston for a Harley Davidson engine, pharmaceutical drugs for Pfizer, on up though subsystem integration, such as a cockpit display for a Sikorsky helicopter, or a complete point of sale product, like a laptop PC.

The term *"job shop"* is used less often these days, but it was *the* term a couple decades ago, when large manufacturing companies would outsource specific tasks and/or items in the production of their products. Even straight assembly labor could be *"offloaded,"* and materials kits would be provided by the OEM (Original Equipment Manufacturer) to external manufacturing companies for processing. These shops would mirror the factory floor for a quick and seamless outsourcing of internal manufacturing. Many contract manufacturers were—and still are—created this way.

Larger scale shops add high speed, automated equipment that can be run on multiple shifts (utilization), supporting a broad customer base. The volumes produced by the OEM may not justify such an expense. Test and verification equipment also follows this logic.

Some companies specialize in a specific process or skill, creating a niche market. A special ability, equipment, or service within the proximity of a few strategic clients can create significant opportunities.

The term *"outsourcing"* also applies to business operations, where a company may hire a third party to perform business tasks, such as IT, accounting, or a customer call center. This study focuses on the manufacturing content of outsourcing, although it does touch on engineering functions, as you will see in the section on ODM Services *(See the glossary for definitions of this and other abbreviations).*

Consignment shops employ an operational strategy where they receive the component level or raw materials from the customer to manufacture higher level assemblies. They typically perform tasks of assembly and/or packaging of products. The advantage of these shops is they provide a standby work force at the ready, while typically operating at lower internal manufacturing costs than the OEM. The supplier achieves this by having lower facility costs and overhead costs on its staff (indirect costs) and typically pays lower wages to its employees (direct cost).

Many consignment shops are located in neighboring *economic zones*, such as Mexico (this is a North American perspective), offering a tremendous advantage in cost over domestic rates in the high rent, technology parks. This is attractive to companies looking to outsource more repetitive, higher volume production and establish materials logistics to those factories. When located in or near technology centers and cities, shops typically cater to prototypes, specialty services, and short run production—where the needs of service and flexibility offset the savings of going further away.

Three Real World Examples:

An OEM company in southern California manufactures cable TV boxes. While this type of electronic assembly is not the most complex to manufacture, it does involve some long lead time components, custom plastic parts, cable assemblies, etc. The Printed Circuit Board Assembly (PCBA) is outsourced to CMs in a consignment fashion, where the OEM supplies the material kits. The OEM avoids the large capital expenditure of setting up a PCB assembly line and staff it, and the subsequent need to efficiently utilize these assets with only a few products to be manufactured. The boxes are made in relatively high volume: 500 to 2000 per kit. The use of several Northern Mexico CMs creates competition for the already low labor costs, and lowers risk of availability by building products at two suppliers when demand is high. While the management of the material has its internal costs, the infrastructure is preexisting, as the OEM manufactures the final assembly in house and has staff and systems in place to handle supply chain execution. The controlling of the materials also gives the OEM ultimate schedule control, as an incomplete kit cannot be run, and the level of the OEM's finished goods can be manipulated via controlling the CM's ability to manufacture. Finally, downtime between demand swings is at no cost to the OEM.

"Day planners" are rapidly being replaced by PDAs. Yet there is still demand for the "hard copy" little scheduling books. Inside the books are various sections and dividers. The final assembly of these planners is very labor intensive, though it requires very little skill or equipment. Again, the Mexico model is a good one. The materials are heavy, typically packaged on pallets. They can be cost effectively trucked across the border and stored right at the CM. The assembly is done by releasing purchase orders, which schedules the labor content. The CM assembles the planners and they are packaged on pallets and trucked back over the border to a logistics center for distribution to retail outlets.

This model works well for all. The freight cost of the materials is insignificant compared to the amount of money saved on storage and labor to assemble the planners. The CM enjoys a profitable piece of business for next to no investment. Benches and human resources are all that is required, plus some space for the inventory. While the CM may be focused on some other market (i.e., cable assemblies), this business's earnings help gobble up the overhead expense and fills otherwise idle capacity.

A Micro Electronics in Southern New Hampshire maintains a "Clean Room" assembly facility staffed with highly skilled and certified solder technicians. The company is small, about 10 people, and not much space is required. Larger OEMs, specifically defense contractors, utilize this niche capability to outsource prototype and production assembly requirements. The labor rates are very high, resulting in a profitable scenario with minimal utilization of assets. The OEM has even higher rates due to location, benefits, and other overhead, so the costs are still attractive, even though the primary reasons are skill, service, and location.

Turnkey shops procure and manage the materials required to fill customer orders. Once called a *time and material* model, turnkey manufacturing allows for the subcontractor/vendor to also make a profit on the material portion of the finished product. This comprises the majority of today's OEM / CM relationships.

For turnkey electronics assembly (things with circuit boards), **the material cost is typically +/-70% of the final sell price of the assembly.** For the EMS industry, this is the rule of thumb. The remaining +/- 30% contains the *Value Add* and profit. Value Add is all of the direct and indirect costs over and above material cost, including labor, overhead, freight, scrap, etc., and profit. The higher the product's volume (and simpler its design), the higher the ratio of material vs. value add (*read: the lower the profit margin*).

Turnkey manufacturing creates a cash flow challenge for the CM, as inventory must be purchased up front, processed through the factory, and then turned back into cash when the customer pays the bill. This skyrockets revenue and profit dollars (not percentage), however.

Turnkey manufacturers also need more staff and systems, such as an MRP (Materials Requirements Planning) system to purchase and schedule materials, as well as having a quality system to handle defective material and ensure regulatory compliance, when applicable. Larger companies have full blown supply chain management teams with commodity specialists to negotiate and "channel" component level items. Also, sophisticated stocking and bond programs can be employed, where the business volume is enough to interest the supply base.

A consignment strategy is often used as a pathway to a turnkey scenario for start up CMs, building the business and absorbing the overhead without the cash strains of managing inventory. A mix of the two strategies can be done as well, and if handled right, can be an excellent business strategy.

Two Examples:

Foxconn is the largest EMS provider in the world. Based in Taiwan, they employ upwards of 300,000 people and have annual revenues over $40 billion. With factories world wide, they market a local presence to their customers for new product introduction, then can migrate volume manufacturing to low-cost facilities located around the globe. Foxconn is also the manufacturer of the iPod for Apple. They have two dedicated factories in China churning out millions of iPods annually. This "focus factory" or "captive work force" exemplifies the optimal, most OEM-like manufacturing scenario, allowing for a continuous workflow and optimized assembly line that manufactures the same products over and over. Statistical Process Control, Lean Manufacturing, as well as sophisticated Supply Chain Execution strategies can all be employed to bolster efficiency, quality, and the bottom line.

Smaller CMs face multiple customers with a mix of products to be manufactured. Encore Manufacturing, of Springfield, MA, with a $50–$100 million revenue range, is a "Top 100" EMS provider. In addition to Springfield, they have a facility in Tijuana, Mexico. To achieve their revenue goals, they must service dozens of customers. Within each customer there are multiple products moving through their lifecycles. These products also vary in the required level of tests, inspection, and documentation; some are for the medical industry, while others are for military and aerospace, telecom, etc.

The factory must be set up in more of a generic model or one with different manufacturing "cells" that can cater to specific industry needs. Prototyping and New Product Introduction (NPI) must also be accommodated along with the downstream volume manufacturing in the same factory. Stable products can migrate to the Tijuana facility, offering customers a low-cost alternative, without losing them to the offshore competition.

This type of CM will enjoy higher margins than the Focused Factory, but they will earn them, as each day can be a scheduling challenge for the factory and its supply base.

While the term "Job Shop" is almost passé, it best describes machining, screw machining, metal fabricators, plastic molding, cable assemblies, etc. These shops are turnkey, because they procure the raw materials to fulfill the customer order, but these materials are typically common from one customer to the next, being assembled or formed to a customer's specifications *(AKA build to print)*.

The job shops typically have a smaller footprint than the larger PCB assemblers, and are more regionally tied to their customer base. And, while their materials model is a turnkey one, they run the reverse financial profile **where +/-70% of the content is the labor, overhead, and profit (Value Add)**. In the EMS model, the 70% is a hard number, typically similar from one shop to the next. In this model, however, one manufacturing company's model can be much different than another, if, for example, there is no debt on the facility or equipment (lower overhead/fixed costs). Process efficiencies can also differ from one shop to another. The result of this is a wider range of pricing between direct competitors, and often, higher profits can be achieved, as they are "un-auditable" by the customers. Also, a higher material markup can contribute to the bottom line, as raw materials are often bought in bulk. Meanwhile, at the turnkey electronics shop, the customers are quibbling over a percentage point of margin or the cost of a piece of hardware, as they can see it in the cost roll up on the bid, or they may have costed the materials themselves.

For the job shops, having the right niche in the right location can be very lucrative. Metal fabricators and machine shops positioned themselves in southern Long Island to support the large DOD OEMs and aircraft component makers. In their day (1980s), these shops flourished with business from Fairchild Aircraft, Grumman, Sperry, and United Technologies, to name a few.

These shops did so well in the '80s that is was rumored that the metal fabrication suppliers to a NY-based aircraft manufacturer gave the purchasing manager's son a "group" wedding gift of a honeymoon, a new car, and a 3 bedroom ranch!

Two real life examples:

Riverside Precision Sheet Metal in New Hampshire is a low to mid volume producer of precision sheet metal parts ("precision" differentiates these shops from those who support the HVAC industry). Employing 12–15 people, the small factory turns revenue in excess of $2 million. Automated punch presses, brakes, and welding capability augment the small work force. Starting out in the family's garage, steady growth over the years has funded multiple additions, increasing physical space to 10,000 sq ft, as well as strategic equipment additions, including a laser "punch" ($250K), and more recently, a high speed electric punch ($300K).This equipment allows them to be competitive on small to moderate production requirements in the local region. For responsiveness, Riverside delivers most of its orders directly to the customer's dock.

Nypro Plastics of Clinton, MA is a very large job shop. Much in the way of the largest EMS providers, they have many facilities around the globe, operate in low-cost manufacturing zones, and market to virtually every industry. Their many locations include support services such as sales and design, and their manufacturing presence accommodates regional needs. Market sectors such as medical are served with the applicable certifications and quality controls.

With respect to the EMS sector, Nypro is large enough to "partner" with the top tier. While this partnership may be nothing more than a statement for marketing, the ability to service the tier one CMs adds credibility as a global player. Additionally, the large CMs can recommend Nypro as their best choice when no plastics supplier is present and vice versa for Nypro, when clients are looking for EMS providers.

The main target for marketing for this type of CM is the OEM designers. Plastics involve special materials and extensive tooling. Typical-

ly, by the time a procurement specialist becomes involved, materials are specified, tooling requirements are defined, and the sourcing decision has been made before the bidding of the requirement.

Service Offerings

In describing the types of CM's above, we profiled the industry with regard to their operating strategy: how they convert raw material into ship level products. The service offerings are the actual skill sets they possess and specific tasks they perform. This is typically the core competence of the company. That, and the style in which these skills are utilized, will define the company's "personality," or marketing footprint. The list is lengthy, but the most common are as follows:

Metal Fabricators are a $40 billion market space in North America alone, catering to just about every industry. Often, they feed into the Contract Electronics Manufacturing (CEMs/EMS) companies that do system integration or *box build* for the OEMs.

As profiled in the previous example, this is a capital equipment intensive business, making the outsourcing decision an easy one for the OEM.

Metal fabricators have several sub-industry classifications: *Stamping*—like car doors or snow shovels; *Fabrication* involves punching, bending, welding, finish, and light assembly, typically for electronics; *Slide Forming* (springs, coils, etc.), *Spinning, and Roll Forming* are other unique processes.

Machining is separated out of the "flat stock" world, and is also capital equipment intensive: milling, drilling, and the traditional lathe, are all employed to create unique metal components.

Plastics molding creates the cases, housings and bezels for all of the electronic stuff we buy, and more. The automotive industry uses many plastic parts, as does the toy industry, etc.

Mr. McGuire was on to something when he gave the career tip to Benjamin in *"The Graduate."*

One of the key things about plastics is that in order to form a shape, you must create a mold for that shape. The molding machines are not only an expensive capital equipment investment—making outsourcing an easy decision—but also the cost, engineering and lead time to create the mold make for an early outsourcing decision in the product development cycle.

The chemical make up of the plastics also supports *staying out of that game,* as environmental compliance can create unneeded business risks for the OEM. The OEM has the end products to deal with, as they do not biodegrade, and new legislation on WEEE, for example, makes the OEM responsible for their ultimate disposal.

Overseas, we see more vertical integration, where the EMS company and the Original Design for Manufacture (ODM) companies will take on the plastics and other subassemblies, keeping control of the product and the profits.

Pharmaceutical—The making of drugs is at $2 billion and growing. Once the drugs are approved, the profitability of a pharmaceutical's manufacturing (cost of goods vs. sell price) can almost be comparable to software. As one supply chain VP stated, "It's like printing money." But it's never enough. Raw materials, as well as outsourced processing of the final products, are scrutinized to maximize profits. Offshore, low-cost regions are looked at and evaluated. And when one of these OEMs lets go of its manufacturing, there can be a more than significant impact from a hiccup in quality.

Dozens of deaths from the blood thinner Heparin were traced to a subcontractor in China, where an inferior product was consciously substituted for the sake of profits. We have recently seen other examples of this in baby food, toothpaste, as well as lead paint in children's toys. But when it comes to the pharmaceutical industry, the controls and procedures that are put in place (or should be), create a perception that this should never happen. Yet, for the sake of cost reduction and profit maximization, the low bid gets a good look. Sometimes, *too* good a look...

This is not to say outsourcing of this process is a bad idea or certain regions are a bad place to outsource to. The pharmaceutical industry is growing and the need to outsource is there, from a business perspective of capital investment and available capacity. As it continues to grow, it must be carefully managed as the margin for error is much tighter here than in other industries.

The common denominator of the above industries is they require a major capital equipment investment to perform their respective manufacturing tasks in a build to print environment.

The **garment** industry sector deals with "soft parts," as they are called. More than just clothing, products such as automotive interiors are mass produced on automated assembly lines. In this industry, however, one typically envisions sweat shops in Bangladesh and China where workers manually sew name brand sneakers and clothing. These are very real conditions, but the industry is evolving. As capital equipment outpaces human labor and produces higher, more consistent quality, a more technical approach is emerging. High speed equipment is now present in these low-cost regions, outpacing the "sweat shop" environment. The percentage of the automated shops is small, however, as the capital equipment market is selling thousands of machines, while the companies in operation are in the tens of thousands. How far it takes us is not clear, but it is obvious that the ability to start a company with cheap labor is much easier than taking the capital equipment road. China leads this industry:

Statistics show that China's textile and garment industries exported 52.1 billion U.S. dollars worth of products in 2000. The export of ready-made clothes totaled 36.1 billion U.S. dollars, 18.1 percent of the world's total.
    -2002 "People's Daily" report

General Assembly, Electromechanical Assembly, and Cable Harness are service offerings requiring less capital investment and are thus easier to get started in. Some of these serve as the off load shops to larger CMs and OEMs. Like the garment industry, benches, stools, people, and a limited amount of equipment can launch you into business. While general assembly can take on jobs like the Day Planner scenario previously mentioned, tools and mechanical skills are required for electromechanical assembly. The Cable and Harness arena can also be easily accessed with limited equipment, but a technical core competence is required to create efficient and reliable products. Also, the turnkey nature of cable assemblies requires materials planning and cash flow to support slow asset turns, as the materials are typically bought in bulk. This industry also lends itself to other assembly, including system level assembly. It is very much like the EMS industry, without the massive inventory commitment.

Electronics Assembly is the largest Industry, and is referred to as the EMS (Electronic Manufacturing Services) industry. These are people who make your iPod, laptop, microwave oven, and garage door opener. This sector comes in around $160–$170 billion annually (plus ODM as depicted below) and has seen a consistent growth rate of about 20% per year, according to *iSuppli Corp.*, an industry consulting group, as well as others.

Though enormous, the top ten companies gobble up about 70% of the revenue, leaving *just* $50 billion or so, for the rest of the market. When looking at *iSuppli's* top 100 EMS providers list, the revenues quickly drop and are sub $30 million per year at the bottom of the list. As far as the rest of the pack, according to the major component distributors, there are about 1000 EMS providers in North America that spend over a million dollars on materials annually. This number fluctuates annually, as dozens appear and disappear, while others are consumed in mergers and acquisitions.

The services of the EMS industry, for the most part, involve the assembly of circuit boards, and often the higher level integration of them, into final, ship level products. For any real production volumes, automated component placement equipment is required. These machines rapidly and accurately place components on the surface of the circuit card, which has been pre-pasted with solder (hence, the term "Surface Mount," or "SMT"). Other major capital equipment includes test systems, including environmental stress screening (ESS) and "burn in" chambers for long test cycles.

Small and large EMS companies alike can create a *virtual factory* scenario, allowing the OEM to have zero manufacturing capabilities. All manufacturing activity, including finished goods warehousing, shipment, and a repair/return depot, can be located at the contract manufacturer. This is sometimes referred to as a *fulfillment model*.

The EMS sector is extremely competitive, as the consumer electronics boom has spawned massive, low-cost factories around the globe to support its voluminous demand. Accompanied with the previously mentioned 70/30 rule, the EMS sector sees very low profit margins for its very high revenue numbers—and often periods of loss when the economy shifts.

Rise of the ODM (Original Design for Manufacturing)

Taking things one step further, EMS providers may offer design services or even reference designs for the OEM's use. A specification such as an MP3 player can be provided by the OEM to the CM who will take it from conception, all the way into volume production for the OEM. Additionally, the ODM may offer ready for production designs, such as PC motherboards, that can shorten the development cycle for an OEM bringing a laptop or desktop to market.

While this is the hottest growth sector in contract manufacturing, the profit margin is also low, albeit a few points above the EMS sector, as the products involved are typically consumer electronics to be produced in high volume, offshore, at very low margins.

This market segment represents **another $110+ billion on top of the EMS figures** and is growing at the same rate. And, here again, the top ten takes the majority of the market.

> *"Concentration of revenue among the Top-10 Electronic Manufacturing Services (EMS) providers and Original Design Manufacturers (ODMs) accelerated at a faster-than-expected rate in 2006. In fact, the Top-10 EMS providers alone controlled 70.4 percent, or $111 billion, of the $157 billion market in 2006. The Top-10 ODM providers controlled 72.8 percent, or $72.8 billion, of the $100 billion market in 2006."*
> Source: *"iSuppli"* April 23rd 2007

There are other service offerings we have not covered. Food, for example (human and pet) is created by a manufacturing process. Also, items like toys, cleaning products, and other chemicals can all be manufactured by third parties. In fact, virtually all manufactured items can be contracted to a third party to be made.

Shapes and Sizes
The purest, most simple form of contract manufacturing is when an employee takes home work and gets paid separately to do it off site. Thus, the work has been offloaded to a third party. Shapes and sizes of contract manufacturing companies range from the **garage shop** with a lathe, on up to the $40 billion Foxconn, employing hundreds of thousands of people world wide.

Within each service offering the competition is fierce. What differentiates one shop from the other, aside from size, is typically minimal. A machine shop is a machine shop. There are some special processes one shop may possess, but the differentiators are typically: **location, type of service, and price**. Regional shops will, for the most part, be direct competitors to each other, especially if they are of similar size. Their specialties that separate them can be: *quick turn* prototypes, highly technical testing capability, volume production, a special process (i.e., brazing, EDM welding), etc.

The smaller enterprises can take off load work from OEMs and local, larger CMs. Having a specific skill set, such as being Mil (Military) certified in soldering, or having a special piece of equipment can make the garage shop very attractive to some companies.

As we start to grow the size of these companies, we start to see structure and business being conducted in a more formal sense. Process automation equipment is present, computer systems to run operations, and formal procedures and quality programs start to appear. A lot of these shops (say 10–50 people) cater to the prototype and low/moderate volume production needs of OEMs. Some of these companies can pass a formal quality audit or survey; many can't. Moving further up, we see more equipment, more complimentary services, and certifications like ISO, FDA, FAA, etc. These companies can document and demonstrate their controls and business processes. *Quality Plans* and *Manuals* are present, documenting the processes of manufacturing operations.

The larger these companies get, the more they look alike. A PCB assembler with 3 surface mount lines turning $25 million in revenue will look very similar to another PCB assembler turning $25 million. They require similar equipment to assemble and test and, if in the same region, will compete for, and sometimes share, the same customers.

Some companies may specialize in a process within their industry, such as brazing or welding. The attractiveness of many of these contract manufacturers is that the OEM/customer's design requires the process, but the projected volume of the product does not warrant the capital investment.

The equipment, location, and target market of the contract manufacturer will define its appearance, or *personality*. For example, a $10 million cable and harness manufacturer that specializes in military cables will have beefy, highly tested cables (and test gear) throughout the facility, while a $10 million cable and harness facility that specializes in commercial box build will have smaller, less rugged cables and harnesses (like the innards of a pinball machine) on the benches, plus automated crimping equipment and volume oriented machinery to maximize throughput.

The largest contract manufacturers have local facilities to support regional manufacturing, as well as locations in global economic zones to offer low-cost, volume production. This is typical of EMS providers, but we also see it in other industries, such as plastics and metal.

While some shops have been around for many years (it seems this would best describe the job shops), the last 10 years has seen many new players and a lot of change to the industry. Automated equipment, documented quality systems, globalization, computing hardware and software, and a major change in product demand have redefined the manufacturing industry. Yet some, like the small machine shop, appear to be frozen in time, with vintage systems and processes that still work just fine (for them).

Markets Served

As mentioned above, the target market of the CM will also help define its shape. **Consumer electronics**, for example, would have high volume, low-cost factories churning out plastics, screens and electronics. It takes a high level of automation to support the cell phone industry, for example, which cranks out 250 million cell phones a year. Nokia's in-house production alone makes six cell phones per second.

After the boom (or ka-boom), **telecom** still managed to crank out $41 billion in product in 2007. The attractiveness to the EMS industry is the circuit boards: big, complex, beautiful, and godly expensive, circuit boards. The EMS companies' surface mount machines are a perfect match for the big server boards, covered with thousands of dollars of components. Some boards exceed $5000 in material content alone. In addition to the material costs, there is typically a high level of testing and possible box build, or final level assembly. These accounts can be risky, as we have learned, but in general, the start up telecom poses the higher risk scenario. To support this style of business, the CM must have a solid EMS infrastructure and quality system. Precision machines and expensive test gear are required, plus the cash to acquire large blocks of inventory.

Bio tech and bio sciences is a growing market segment. Here we see more system level products such as analyzers and processing equipment. While there are opportunities for the EMS provider, the job shops, and the CMs who are more into system integration will find a better match up to their outsourcing content.

The **military/aerospace** market segment has enjoyed a huge upswing business with the US waging wars for many years. The subcontractors that cater to the DOD contractors (OEM's that make war toys) are flourishing. The job shops do especially well in this market swing because they do not have offshore competition, and there are many mechanical parts in everything from tanks to aircraft to missiles.

Military compliance has given way to commercial and aviation quality certificates, but the style of a military shop, more often than not, is not considered lean, catering to the rugged nature of the products the shop produces.

Everyone loves **industrial controls**. This industry is a sweetheart to the CM. In this industry, the technology is stable when compared to just about everything else. This means very few, if any, engineering changes occur to disrupt daily life. Also, the technology to build the products is typically basic. New products are introduced and then stay for a much longer time than in, say, the telecom world. And the volumes are so low that "offshore" doesn't make sense: it's more important to have product available when the customer wants it. Perhaps the best part about these customers is they typically have been around for a long time and are not the ranting and raving types. And they have lots of cash. So, do we have the perfect customer? Possibly . . .

New analysis from Frost & Sullivan on EMS provider opportunities in the **medical device industry**, reveals that the North American EMS medical device market earned revenues of $3.79 billion in 2006 and estimates this to reach $8.09 billion in 2013.

Medical device manufacturing is the new rage in North America. Not that is has not been around, but it is a high growth sector, and the quality requirements (QS 13485) make for a smaller playing field. Offshore suppliers are approved for medical devices as well, pointing the high volume, lower cost products east.

Automotive provides the volumes of consumer electronics, but contrary to the EMS ODM model of vertical integration, less than 25% of an automobile is manufactured by the maker. Components and subsystems, such as ignition systems, taillights, interior liners, and power seats all are subcontracted to third parties, rendering the car maker to be a chassis manufacturer and systems integrator, so to speak.

While the volumes are huge, the logistics are tight, as the car manufacturers will not allow for downtime or advance purchase of any significant finished goods from the supply base. The penalties for not delivering are so severe, in fact, that a NH-based aircraft charter company would be hired to fly light bulbs in via private aircraft—while the tractor trailer made its way on the ground—to avoid a line down situation.

A great industry to be a part of, but as a subcontractor, one must remember who carries the big stick.

Technology

In order to assess the technology gains in the contract manufacturing industry, you must look to the Capital Equipment Manufacturers. While necessity is the mother of invention, the needs of the CM industry are listened to, and then satisfied by, their capital equipment manufacturers.

Technology advancements created by a CM are infrequent, if at all.

Most advances are in robotic/process automation equipment and material handling. Also, automatic test and verification equipment, including optical inspection have increased throughput and enhanced factory cycle times.

EM Asia's "Innovation 2007 Award" went to Elcoteq for their end to end service model. Their ability to introduce products, then migrate them to the proper logistical manufacturing facility, was considered best in class. The key fact here is there is no new technology created, just the proper application of available technology, business and process control, and service to the customer. The resulting "package" is award winning, but it is only the use of existing technology that is award winning, not the creating of any new technology.

Each service sector can be reviewed for examples of technological advancements over the years. Machine shops went high tech years ago with CNC (computer numeric control). More recent advancements are in automating the upstream processes that feed the machines, with special software that can be downloaded directly to the very machines that will do the given manufacturing process. CAD, or Computer Aided Design, results in CAM, or Computer Aided Manufacturing, where special files are created for specific machine processes, eliminating time-consuming equipment programming as well as the *opportunity for error* in those manual processes. These advancements apply to virtually all of the service sectors in contract manufacturing.

Metal fabricators saw lasers radically improve their ability to punch metal. The laser eliminated the need for tooling and could be easily programmed to cut complicated shapes. Changeovers became quick, tooling costs were eliminated, and the ability to create low volume, one-offs was greatly enhanced.

The EMS industry has been revolutionized by high speed automatic component placement machines, with ratings of 40,000+ components per hour (actual times approach half that). The manufacturers of this equipment supply thousands of such machines each year, as do the manufacturers of automated inspection and in line test equipment, all with the smallest possible footprints on the factory floor.

The speed of these machines has finally outpaced human labor with respect to cost. In Mexico, factory workers' wages were $1.25 hr in the early 2000s. The older, Through Hole assembly line could not run at less cost than a team of assemblers, when considering the cost of maintenance on the machines and the electricity to run them.

Similar advancements in the garment industry have been made as well, where the larger shops are now considering automation over manual labor. Large tables with automated cutting tools can be programmed to cut out an automobile interior, or multiple articles of clothing. The technology revolves around the handling of *"soft parts,"* where, rather than assembly, there is cutting, punching of holes, and matching of fabric.

3. Industry Historical Overview

Origins / Trends

During the Cold War, the DOD created a market sector that flourished. In Connecticut alone, there was Avco Lycoming (jet engines), Hubble (Aerospace), Pratt and Whitney (jet engines) Hamilton Standard (avionics), Sikorsky (helicopters), and Norden Systems (avionics, weapon delivery systems), to name a few. The suppliers to these companies were the essence of contract manufacturing, as they supplied such services as machining, metal fabrication, cable assembly, and off load production services. These products were typically Mil-Spec, and thus not cheap, enabling the subcontractors to make handsome profits.

Back in the '60s, Space Craft Industries in Huntsville, Alabama, started out like other small companies, positioning themselves in an industrial zone of large aerospace / DOD manufacturers to support their subcontract needs. As the company grew, it diversified, taking on more and more commercial work and adding more facilities. Eventually, they lost the formal name and became just "SCI."

For consumer products, we looked offshore, with televisions, stereos, and appliances being made in Japan and Taiwan. As technological advances were made, we saw other consumer products become laden with electronic controls. To iron your clothes, you now had a device that not only got hot, but had a motion sensor and timer that would shut itself off, if tipped over or left unattended. And our coffee pots now could be programmed to make the coffee while we slept. As the digital age came upon us, the need for manufacturing capacity of these items grew, and the electronics manufacturing services industry was born.

When we left the 1980s, we were just getting introduced to the PC. Hard drives were large at 40 megabytes. Monitors were amber. We listened to our music on vinyl and tape. We did not have cell phones. And our cars did not have air bags, engine management systems, anti-lock brake systems, or automatic stability control. This was all about to change . . .

A New Period, Not an Era . . .

Now, the planet is carpeted with electronic gadgets. The factories that support this ever growing market dominate this study. But, before we continue on with how we got here, let's fast forward a million years or so . . .

> The archaeological dig by the planet's next highest species is attempting to figure out the reason for the sudden extinction of the human race—after such a short existence. Did it melt down? Overheat? Blow up? The dig reveals the "stripe," like the black one of the dinosaurs. But, this one is not black, but a sort of grey and beige, littered with plastic.
> "Hey look! I found another one of these little devices with a tiny keyboard . . ."
> "Tag it as an 'Input Device' and put it on the pile over there."
> "Hey! Here is another one of those little gadgets with the circle and the earphones. I swear, everyone must have had one of these."
> "Maybe that's the way their leader talked to them. Toss it in the 'Output Device' pile."
>
> This period in the planets evolution will be just that. A period; it was way too short to be an era. It shall be called the **Gizmozoic Period**, when the planet was obsessed with little gadgets that did things to make life easier.

The factories that support the Gizmo market proliferated in the '90s. Riding this rollercoaster over the next 15 years witnessed personal computing, the handheld electronics boom, the automotive industries migration to "smart" safety, suspension, and engine management systems, surfing the web, the rise and implosion of dot coms and telecoms, cell phone mania, and the rage of miniature digital media devices.

Real life:
It was back in the early '90s, when the PC wars began with Packard Bell, HP, IBM, and Dell. Dell went to an outsourcing model and awarded SCI the turnkey manufacturing of the 386 and 486 PC. At the time, SCI was the largest "board stuffer" in the word, with revenues of $1.5 billion.

The program was to make 400+ per day of each, $100+ million per year, ship directly to the point of sales, manage returns and repairs, etc. (fulfillment model). The pricing would yield about a 2% profit. Purchase orders were cut to schedule the products, but there was no master contract in place (at least in the beginning).

To ramp up, the corporate office summoned other SCI facilities to make the motherboards. Their New Hampshire facility would make the 386MHZ motherboards (in-sourcing), 400+ per day, sent via air freight to Huntsville, Alabama, where the PCs would be assembled and shipped the following day. Two other facilities would support the 486 motherboards in the same fashion. All component level materials were scheduled, and production was up and running within a few weeks. After a few months, Dell decided they were just going to sell 486s and, as fast as it started, it all ended for the NH plant. The other facilities continued on with Dell shipping directly to SAM's club (there was no Fry's, Best Buy, or Circuit City back then) for point of sale. The 30-day warranty was perfectly executed by many students needing a PC to do their term papers, then, returning them—to SCI—for a full refund. Meanwhile, the New Hampshire facility had to deal with a large amount of excess material, arguing with their "customer," the box build facility in Huntsville, who in turn dealt with Dell, but had no contract.

Why would a CM take on such a volatile program with virtually no profit to be made? While there were certainly risks, SCI leveraged this business to fund a high volume, massive "box build" facility. This would, in theory, create the capacity to support continued growth in this new, emerging market. SCI saw this capability as the future.

Ten years later, these facilities were everywhere, both operational and shut down—depending upon which market swing you were on.

CMs looking to boost revenue and jump start business in new regions would (and still do) take on entire (OEM) factories in a divestiture of a product line or manufacturing facility. The fate of these new facilities, however, was often unclear.

Growth into Market Segment

SCI's vision was correct. Factories supporting complete, end to end manufacturing needs sprang up all over the globe. Over the last ten years the growth of the EMS industry has created a new customer for the downstream supply chain of the component distributors as well as the job shops.

The EMS industry, in total, is now its own market segment, yet it has no product or IP. This growing trend creates marketing challenges for the supply base.

Getting "designed in" at the OEM can carry itself through to the CM for strategic components in the design. But, the distributors who carry the components are competing at the CM's door for the business, rather than winning the business with the engineers at the OEM. There are "registrations" that can direct business through the proper channels, but more and more, the OEMs will allow, and sometimes look to the EMS provider for, commodity sourcing. Quality plans and documented supplier qualification procedures at the EMS provider enable the OEM to provide freedom to the EMS company in choosing their supplier for their subcontract needs, such as sheet metal fabrication, cable assemblies, etc.

Winning a customer can now be a two step process for the downstream supplier. First, working with the OEM to support their initial design, building prototypes during the development phase, then subsequently winning the follow-on production. If the OEM outsources production, the job shop must now get in front of the EMS provider, become a qualified supplier, and be competitively priced, all over again.

Sometimes, sources are directed by the OEM that has the confidence in the quality and comfort in the price, meaning the EMS provider doesn't have to reinvent the wheel. The EMS provider will typically accept this because they get an *agreed to* markup on the components, and, any downstream quality or delivery issues with that supplier would be considered *induced* by the customer. But the job shop must remain on top of the relationship with the EMS provider, as they can become a political football when issues arise, and the EMS provider may ask the OEM for permission to quote these products to other sources when being pressured for a cost reduction.

As the EMS sector has enjoyed a steady 20% per year growth rate (until recently), the job shops, as well as the component suppliers, have had to change their strategy to support the EMS providers, rather than expect to be "handed off" to the facility where the products will be built.

Another trend in the young EMS sector: buying a competitor or taking on an OEM's factory to boost revenue faster than any other sales cycle could.

Mergers and Acquisitions

With 48 completed EMS transactions in 2008, the year falls short of the 51 recorded transaction in 2007. From those, EMS consolidations were the most common transaction in 2008, with 19 consolidations (40% of total activity). While 2007 had the same number of consolidations, those represented only 38% of that year's activity.
-Evertiq

"Growth via acquisition" is a proven model. Ironically, the job shop style companies are rarely seen buying each other up. Why? Perhaps it is because the job shops generate higher profits on lower revenues, making the owners more complacent (and the "owners" are typically one person, not an investment group or publicly traded company). So, when you are banking 25% of revenue, there is no hurry to get to $100 million in sales. On the other hand, if you are netting 2%–3%, and have to answer to the board . . .

SCI, now Sanmina-SCI grew through many acquisitions, the final name of the company being perhaps the most famous acquisition. Bigger yet, was the more recent acquisition of Solectron by Flextronics: number two buying number four in a futile effort to catch number one, the now $50+ billion Foxconn.

> ***First, SCI, where Davy buys Goliath:***
> *The SCI growth model was to acquire small to medium sized CMs in strategic areas, then introduce more business through increased sales or interdivisional needs, simultaneously beefing up the infrastructure to handle larger customers. The overhead costs were, at least, partially absorbed by the preexisting revenue stream as the division morphed. Over time, SCI grew up to be the largest CM in the world with a low-cost, low margin business model. Competitors like Solectron and Flextronics grew up, too, eventually taking away SCI's "number one" bragging rights and establishing the "mega-tier": the multi-billion dollar EMS providers.*
>
> *The smaller Sanmina also made it to the mega-tier, and had a model where they catered to higher technology clients with special needs and could thus post higher margins. The two were well matched for a merger and to take over the number one slot at $14 billion. But the smaller Sanmina had a better balance sheet and bought the bigger player, SCI, that was running on fumes with their low-cost, high volume business model and massive, underutilized factories.*

Not just the big dogs get to play this game. Smaller companies just make smaller acquisitions. A $100 million CM looking to strategically grow might scout acquisition targets in the $10–$20 million range. This would provide a nice increase to revenue, be affordable to the business, and create a presence in a new geographical location. Some choose larger bites:

> **Example:**
> In 2004, CTS Electronics, acquired SMTEK International; both companies held top 100 EMS provider status. In the deal, CTS increased its revenue by $100 million and gained strategic facilities. In Massachusetts, however, the SMTEK facility was closed, transferring the existing business to the nearby Londonderry, NH, CTS facility.

In theses mergers there is always a shake out. First, one must understand the driving force behind the event. A company may have unprofitable facilities, or be a good logistical/business target for takeover. While the fact is that no one's job may be safe after a merger, the reality is that many more jobs might have been at risk prior to it. The above facility that was closed was actually Century Manufacturing, which was sold to SMTEK a couple of years prior. That sale had a motivating force, as there were rumors of financial trouble for Century in the months prior to the sale. The SMTEK purchase perhaps delayed the inevitable. Upon acquisition, a failing facility, division, or strategic piece of business can be merged into another facility making the package viable. As with the divestiture model, the acquiring party is on a timeline to make things profitable. If a facility or division cannot stand on its own, then it risks being consolidated into another facility, being sold off again—typically to a smaller player trying to do the same thing—or being shut down.

> **More real life:**
> ACT Manufacturing absorbed Motorola's modem manufacturing plant in the late '90s, taking the assets and staff of the facility. The modems were in their sunset years and volumes were in decline. The division could no longer sustain the higher overheads of the OEM and no new products were being introduced to utilize the increasing available capacity. Once the divestiture was complete, ACT then introduced other customer programs to the facility to bring profitability and maintain overhead absorption.

Sweco buys Flextronics ODM unit
SWECO's industrial consulting arm SWECO PIC has acquired the wireless product development unit of Flextronics ODM Finland Oy, with 16 employees in the Finnish city of Kuopio.
-*Evertiq, June 01 2007,*

In the above announcement, SWECO takes on a Flextronics ODM unit. Read between the lines: there are 16 employees with a core competence of wireless technology development. This business unit may have come with an earlier acquisition, or was created based on a need or projected need in the region. It obviously was not contributing to the bottom line or a needed capability for another Flextronics facility.

On the corporate level, post merger, there are overhead and executive functions that get consolidated. First, finance, then marketing, and so on. It may take months for the dust to settle, but the bottom line is the bottom line. The buying company has increased its revenue and must now make it all work on the balance sheet. "Restructuring," as it's called, is inevitable, and the industry's daily news attempts to keep the tally of this constant shuffling of the deck.

And mergers and acquisitions don't come without issues. As one VP of a top 100 EMS provider put it, *"Don't think of us as a $100 million CM—think of us as five, $20 million CMs..."* Even after a successful merger, CMs with multiple facilities have to face the fact that these companies are different from each other. What happens next is up to the parent company. Some, other than making sure the overhead and profitability is in line, leave things as they are, having regional facilities operating independently and generating revenues independently, with the parent acting more like a holding company.

Many CMs that grow through acquisition will market their new, multi-facility capability, touting the ability to migrate products to other facilities to make available capacity and/or lower costs. But, this may be very difficult if they have completely different structures, systems, and processes. To market a common, transferable footprint, changes must be made. First, the processes and systems must be synchronized for data interchange and the ability to transfer manufacturing processes to another facility. In addition, shop floor layout (to support the processes) and equipment must be made identical, or at least compatible. SCI took the latter approach and morphed all of their acquisitions into the SCI model, including equipment, organization of staff, benefits, Enterprise Resource Planning system (ERP) or MRP system, centralized procurement (where all material was purchased from one office and routed to the facilities to leverage volume pricing), and financial reporting. Each SCI facility was run almost identically.

Neither approach is wrong, unless you market/promote the company counter to the strategy.

> *Jabil Circuit is a top 5 EMS provider. They have a global presence and market the ability to transition any product from an NPI stage to volume production, transitioning the manufacturing to any of their other facilities. A colleague at a multi-billion dollar OEM believes they are among the best at this capability. All facilities have the same data management practices and equipment, so manufacturing process documentation can be transferred from facility to facility.*
>
> *This OEM has worked with many top/mega-tier EMS companies and described transitioning products within another top 5 EMS provider's facilities as a continuous disaster, because the factories came on line through acquisitions and were not changed. Yet, the EMS provider touts seamless production transition as one of their strong core competencies.*

The existing infrastructure of acquired facilities can vary greatly:

SPRINGFIELD, MA (June 4, 2007) *Nu Visions Manufacturing, LLC and Golden Gate Capital, a San Francisco-based private equity firm with $3.5 billion under management, today announced the acquisition of* **Veritek Manufacturing Services, LLC**. *Veritek, based in San Marcos, CA, with additional manufacturing facilities in San Jose, CA, and Longmont, CO, provides electronic manufacturing services ("EMS") to blue chip, medical, defense, gaming and industrial customers. The combined Company will have five manufactur-*

ing facilities in North America, including sites on the East Coast and West Coast as well as a low-cost facility in Mexico. Terms of the deal were not disclosed.
Press Release- Nu Visions, LLC

Nu Visions' (Now Encore Manufacturing) acquisition came after Veritek's acquisition of DDI's Colorado manufacturing plant. DDI, focused in the printed circuit board business, decided to revert back to its core competence of raw board manufacturing (read between the lines) and sold the EMS division to Veritek. This acquisition may have had multiple systems and processes within it.

On the other hand, Nu Visions' Mexico facility was created from scratch, and mirrors the Massachusetts facility. Products from the Springfield facility are easily migrated to Mexico, but they will have to address the new facility's infrastructure for compatibility with the Mexico one to market that capability in the new facilities.

Cisco's "Lean Manufacturing" initiative reduced their EMS supply base, and awarded much of their business to Solectron (others reportedly walking away from the terms). Along with the top line revenue boost, came a pushback of huge amounts of inventory, further crippling Solectron's already tender cash flow. There is speculation that this one customer may have been the last straw for Solectron. Strapped for cash, and with too much tied up in slow moving inventory, selling was the only option for survival. Flextronics had migrated their business toward low-cost manufacturing and the consumer electronics market (including communications and computing). The addition of Solectron helped backfill business in the telecom/higher tech arena, and made a huge revenue leap toward Foxconn.

Growth via acquisition or divestiture is a practice used daily in the industry, creating new EMS companies, as well as growing existing ones. Will this behavior continue? As Foxconn continues clipping along at double digit growth rates, the rest of the industry is compelled to give chase. As the chase ensues, companies look at each other as building blocks for market share. And when the economy shifts, companies can become vulnerable. Low valuation for publicly held firms can make them an acquisition target. Excess capacity can also bring about discussions of merger or partial sell off. If a significant customer has left a gap in capacity, the cycle time to replace it may financially jeopardize the company. As with inventory tying up precious cash, the same holds true for capital equipment. And, as either of these will cripple cash flow, credit issues with the supply base compounds the problem; the already low margins provide a long path to recovery. At the end of the day, acquisition can be a nice exit strategy out of a sticky situation.

Globalization

As we left the last century, the technologies the local CM's produced were the very things that would cut their own throat. Computing and telecommunications equipment were rapidly shrinking the planet.

The ability to communicate in real time is such a given in today's world, that we forget what life was like just fifteen or twenty years ago. There was no e-mail, no Internet to speak of, and no cell phones. A long distance phone call was expensive. For business we used a fax— a video conference was almost unheard of given that the cost of the equipment was in excess of $50,000 and a T1 line was required (if you could get one).

Today, we can Skype with a web cam built into a $400 laptop, IM someone on the other side of the planet, and transfer money around the globe almost as fast. As far away factories came on line, the perception of third world countries building only the cheapest, plastic, toy-like items started to fade. The Far East was open for business and quickly proving itself as a contender for the world's manufactured electronics.

Modern communications and freight logistics have enabled the creation of manufacturing zones around the planet, supplying the world's manufacturing needs. Manufacturing facilities are not only positioned in the lowest cost regions, but anywhere that makes logistical sense in the formula to ensure product availability, competitive prices, and the highest profits. Behind this is the OEM and the mission to be more competitive and reduce "COGS" (Cost of Goods Sold), wherever and however possible.

While we spiked the economy with the telecom boom, there were things in play that would change the way we did business in the following decade. While the first decade discovered the PC, the server, and the cell phone, they were not in vogue unit the late '90s. The laptop also came on the scene, but like the phone, it was heavy and expensive.

As the miniaturization of electronics grew leaps and bounds, the factories around the globe had come up the curve in process control and quality. The subsequent implosion of the telecoms in 2001 left the domestic manufacturing market in shambles, but the available capacity was not the type of capacity needed for the next decade of contract manufacturing. Low cost was the new rage.

The incredible demand for consumer electronics has seen disproportionate growth with respect to other industries such as medical, aerospace, etc. This has facilitated the quick emergence of Foxconn as the world's largest EMS provider. Based in Taiwan (formal name: Hon Hai Precision Company), their factories are predominantly in Asia, with a focus on low-cost, high volume consumer products. They offer not only less expensive manufacturing and supply channels, but have vertical integration, offering the job shop commodities for less—and keeping all profits in house. The other top CMs are giving chase, but with the present formula, and a stronghold on many consumer products such as the iPod, Foxconn continues to increase the gap in market share.

CMs in Recession

CMs have experienced two major recessions in the past ten years. The financial markets show the rise and fall for each economic swing in the timeline trend chart. The first peak, truly a bubble, fired by the telecom industry, which heavily relies on contract manufacturing. The overfunded and under-revenued dot coms imploded, taking the EMS market with it.

The recovery saw handheld electronics and lower cost PCs, including laptops setting the pace for EMS market share. In the second recession, the EMS providers started off weakened, having run on very low margins for the last five years. With each swing, there is a thinning of the herd. The larger companies get acquired, smaller ones tank. The result is a stronger herd, plus a tightening of the supply chain. Lead times are ignored by OEMs, CMs raise rates and get more cautious, and distributors ratchet up their terms. We will cover this in more detail later in this study.

Then, as the next bubble expanded, the good times looked as though they were returning . . .

4. Industry Market Overview

Low-cost Alternatives

After material costs have been revisited over and over, and no more can be squeezed, the OEM's eyes turn offshore. The labor costs in emerging regions are so low, they warrant a look. If the OEM can reduce COGS by an additional 10–15%, that number goes right to the bottom line. On large, steady programs, the cost savings far outweighs the cost of doing business overseas. For smaller programs, there are successes and failures, depending on the product, its needs, and the expertise in managing the effort—on both sides, OEM and contract manufacturer.

Mexico poses another opportunity for the North American OEM, or North American point of sale. Pricing will not be as low as China, Indonesia, or India, but logistics are much better without the need for sea freight, plus the communications are better matched with respect to time zones (especially if you are a California OEM). Large appliances such as televisions, stoves, washers, and dryers are made in Mexico to ship in to the US via truck, avoiding the cost and lead time of ocean freight.

Probably the most infamous low-cost outsourcer is the garment industry. Fashion designer/celebrity line clothes made in sweatshops around the world make for good media stories; the world wants to see how Kate Jackson or Martha Stewart can explain the treatment of the people that are making them rich.

Additionally, the source of demand is shifting. As emerging nations become more industrialized, they establish themselves as a point of sale market, starting with the basics—construction materials and energy—moving on up to industrial controls and telecommunications. Once the infrastructure of a region is built to sustain and grow manufacturing, it eventually emerges as a new market for the very items they are making, as their own people now have money, creating individual demand for consumer products. As the low-cost regions industrialize, competition for the work force ensues (in good times). This raises cost and promotes exploration into the next new region of the lowest available cost to manufacture.

Emerging Regions

Presently, **China** has the lion's share of the global manufacturing market. A concerted effort to industrialize, combined with the explosion of the consumer electronics industry has positioned China to be the world's largest supplier of manufactured goods. And a single supplier, Foxconn (Taiwan), dominates the industry, with revenues exceeding the entire available European market.

> *According to data from China's Ministry of Information Industry, the country imported 10,351 units of surface-mount technology equipment in 2006, 77.5 percent from Japan. Driven by the fast growth in manufacturing products such as handset, notebook computers and digital cameras, China had a total of 20,000 surface-mount technology product lines with 50,000 units of production equipment by the end of 2006. Of that number, 90 percent of the equipment was imported from 2001 to 2006, with an annual growth rate of 27.2 percent.*
> -Amy Wang, Contributing Editor—Electronic News, 8/16/2007

As cities industrialize, they create a large and available work force. Competition sets in, and the work force becomes mobile. Also, the cities start to regulate with regard to the work force and the environment, causing development in newer regions, such as central China, to achieve the lowest possible costs.

Other new regions for manufacturing are emerging to capture the lowest available cost; the largest players are opening facilities, mostly built from scratch.

India is growing with the reports of 20%+ annual increases, which is in line with the industry. The largest OEMs have established a presence there, specifically, the cell phone makers. Now in the same neighborhoods, the CM's show up, looking for the cell phone manufacturers' table scraps to fuel their factories, and gobble up the overhead. From there, they market the cost and presence to the globe. Sound familiar? Remember the aerospace model of the '60s where CMs placed their operations close to the large OEMs and DOD suppliers?

Initially, we saw India emerge as a resource for technical and administrative labor. There are many software companies that provide programming services for about $10 per hour. Also, we see the famous (or infamous) call centers for many companies from credit card providers to technical support. Dell Computer made *The New York Times* with a story on the difficulties when communicating with their tech support, resulting in a losing battle by Dell when challenging the professionalism of the articles. Yet, India has been very successful at luring these businesses away from the US, even with the language barrier and the time difference. So successful, that in Bangalore, an IT development hot bed, an average hotel room can cost up to $700 per night for the business traveler—more than a month's wages for its employees!

Now, with the rise of manufacturing, all business issues, including infrastructure, logistics, legal requirements, etc., are on the table and being dealt with. India is being profiled alongside China as the other dominating force in manufacturing for the foreseeable future. The sheer size of these counties alone warrants the ranking. But, while both are emerging regions (China with about a 10-year jump over India) that must develop their land to support the economic growth, they are both very different. India is a democracy and China is not. Opinions on the pluses and minuses of this vary, some saying that India will be a more familiar setting for business with respect to regulations on doing business and thus be more successful in the long term. Others believe that China's autocratic government has a more "git 'er done" approach and will ensure continued growth. That plus Hong Kong's, Taiwan's and Singapore's business centric demographics make China (and now Malaysia and Vietnam) the "local" low-cost manufacturing zone.

As **Thailand and Malaysia** have now evolved into viable manufacturing locations, **Vietnam** has been sitting virtually untouched, until now . . .

> *According to the Foreign Investment Agency, there are 48 projects totaling US$39.8 billion waiting to come to Vietnam.*
>
> *A large part of this huge source of capital will be poured into hi-tech, thermo-power, real estate and steel projects. Specifically, Taiwan's Foxconn Group will invest $5 billion to build electronic technology parks in several provinces in Vietnam. Pacific Land Limited from Britain plans to invest $1 billion into the Sai Dong, a hi-tech Park in Hanoi.*
>   *VietNamNet Bridge—Aug 2007*

In Europe, we see costs that were in line with US manufacturing now rising due to the lower value of the USD. India and China offer the lowest cost answer globally, but as Mexico serves the US, a local, low-cost scenario has evolved in **Eastern Europe**. With labor and real estate costs much lower than Western Europe, the eastern block countries offer regional service at a large discount, without the logistical challenges of India and China.

> *The European market, as a whole, is approximately $40 billion USD. Fifty percent of that market is supplied via Eastern Europe*.*
>   *-Frost and Sullivan Report—June 2007*

In 2008, MHM Research stated that 85% of the electronics manufactured in Europe are made in Eastern Europe. This shift has taken many of Europe's manufacturing jobs and migrated them a relatively short distance to achieve a low cost-manufacturing model.

The **Dominican Republic/Haiti** is also an emerging (actually, re-emerging, as they used to dominate the clothing industry) region. They offer labor rates as good as, or better than, Mexico, and reside in the eastern time zone, matching the live communications window with companies in the Eastern US. The logistics do not offer trucking, but there is sea freight, and Miami, Florida, is a short flight away. As with any emerging geographical area, the DR has its challenges. Labor, the reason for the attraction to this region, is plentiful, but as with the other young regions, the skilled laborers and technicians are in high demand.

> *The law, known as the Haitian Hemispheric Opportunity Through Partnership Encouragement Act, or HOPE, could create 50,000 jobs in Haiti in the next few years and provide a boost to the hemisphere's most impoverished nation, diplomats and industry leaders say. The law went into effect in March.*
>
> *-Chicago Tribune, June, 2007*

Even the smallest North American CMs have overseas **affiliates** and partners in their marketing portfolio. These CMs use the same *local NPI to offshore production* model as the large CMs, just for smaller opportunities. The local office can also serve as a logistics depot for safety stock, local inspection, and depot repair. Program management also resides locally to support the customer. This carries on through to the large, multi-national EMS firms, with massive factories in low-cost regions. They will typically establish local NPI (New Product Introduction) centers with moderate volume production capability in the high rent district, then transition volume manufacturing strategically around the globe when costs need to be driven downward.

> ***Example:***
> *Circuit Service Inc., of Wheeling, Illinois, is a top 100 EMS provider with revenues in the $50 million range. Catering to the industrial controls, gaming and medical markets, some products were offshore candidates. Rather than partner with an offshore CM, Circuit Service built its own manufacturing plant in China. The ability to*

> create the facility from the ground up allowed them to mirror the Wheeling facility in process, equipment, and systems, making for a smooth production transition across the pond.
>
> (As this study was written, CSI was acquired by Creation Technologies, of Canada.)

China maintains a significant lead on most of these regions. Also, we see a lot of vertical integration, which supports the ODM models. Companies can design and tool for plastics—and most aspects of manufacturing—in house, right down to the packaging of a consumer product. As mentioned earlier, this bolsters profits, keeping the profit that would be paid to a subcontractor as part of their purchase price of the components. The slight increase in the bottom line greatly enhances the financial position of the company; remember, we are dealing with single digit margins.

> 49 of the largest EMS companies reported -2.0% profit for 2005. The ODMs surveyed fared better, posting 6–7% profits.
>
> April 2007: Celestica posts a $34 million loss for Q1 and Flextronics ends their year at $18.9 billion, with a 2.5% profit.
> - iSuppli

In other contract manufacturing industries, we see similar statistics. The garment industry uses low-cost, manual labor in the same vein as the electronics workers. There is a great amount of competition in this industry, resulting in tight margins.

> Currently, 45,000 garment businesses in China produce more than 310 articles of clothing per second and make a profit of 60,000 U.S. dollars every minute.
> Peoples Daily, date unknown

Although still operating at higher margins, metal forming and machining continue to see offshore competition driving prices down, eroding profits and revenue, especially on volume production.

Example:
In 2000, American Power Conversion of Rhode Island established overseas manufacturing to become more competitive in consumer electronics. Their engineering remains local, as does some of their manufacturing. A new product involves a small metal chassis. The local cost is about $21 (winning bid by Riverside Precision Sheet Metal). The target cost is less than $10 and will be achieved in India where 2–4 million of these will be made. The first 1,000–3,000 units will be made on shore, as the local shop cannot touch the offshore price.

EMS Conundrum—The ODM

The lines of demarcation are vanishing. Contractually, the traditional CM was the carpenter in the relationship—not the architect. The liabilities were clear: the performance of the product was never guaranteed, just the workmanship. Now, the ODM changes all that by taking on product development and post sales support. Leaving just the marketing to the OEM.

The **ODM** trend has brought contract manufacturing full circle—from breaking the vertical integration model at the OEM, to reinventing it in a purchased commodity. Originally, we outsourced the assembly content to a CM whose costs were lower because they had no product marketing or product development. That was the sales pitch from the CM. Each service provider could win the argument that the customer/OEM should not be in their business (manufacturing). Within the CM, the same rules applied. If you were a board stuffer, you were not a sheet metal house. Sometimes a company might diversify into a "sister" trade. You may have a sheet metal house that offers machining, but as it gets larger, it typically separates into different divisions. In the same way, PCB assemblers might have cable assembly capability.

Now, especially in Asia, the contract manufacturers are reversing the model to bolster the bottom line. First, engineering services are offered, then tooled parts such as plastics and metal are added.

Finally, reference designs are offered—PC motherboards, for example. This offering can eliminate design cycle times and costs for their OEM customers.

Another variation on this theme is the **JDM** approach, or "Joint Design for Manufacture." In this model the OEM participates in the design, rather than just "selecting one" the ODM offers. There is sufficient in-house design and vertically integrated capabilities to bring the product to life at the CM (or ODM).

The low costs of operations in Asia and now India result in large, vertically integrated factories replete with comprehensive engineering staffs. The cost model is still lower than an in-house design effort by the OEM, although one must consider true cost (TCO, Total Cost of Ownership, or TCA Total Cost of Acquisition), as well as risk.

The ODM/JDM overlap creates a gray area for EMS companies. Foxconn, for example, is listed as the largest EMS company, and provides manufacturing services for products, as earlier mentioned, like Apple's iPod. Yet, they are fully staffed and support OEM's new product development and introduction in a JDM role. If a company is looking to create a PC, they can also use one of Foxconn's motherboards—making them an ODM. One step further, you, as a consumer, can go online and buy a Foxconn motherboard through a retailer; can you say, "OEM"?

Even as electronics manufacturers have stumbled in recent years, one company, Taiwan's Hon Hai Precision Industry Co., more well known as Foxconn, has blown past the competition to become the top player in the industry.

Hon Hai "is the key reason Flextronics and Solectron merged," says Byron Wu, China research manager for electronics market watcher iSuppli Corp. in an interview with Business Week. *Hon Hai's sales jumped 44% in 2006, to $40 billion, which is more than the combined revenues of its three nearest rivals, Flextronics, Solectron, and Jabil Circuit. Profits for Hon Hai climbed 47%, to $1.8 billion, for the*

year. And its stock has been up 52% in the past 12 months. According to Business Week *the reason why Hon Hai is getting along better than its rivals is that it makes about one-third of its own components, everything from printed circuit boards and connectors to the casings for iPods. According to Macquarie Securities Ltd. that helps boost Hon Hai to keep better cost control and cut more profitable deals. The comparable figure for competitors is under 10 percent.*
  -Evertiq

As the boundaries vanish, the low margin, EMS provider is now pulled across the line into the high stakes OEM game. In May of 2007, Acer Inc., a Taiwanese laptop maker, notified its three EMS/ODM suppliers, requesting they participate (financially) in the litigation process of a patent infringement suit filed by HP. According to the *Economic Daily News* (EDN), the suppliers included Hon Hai, AKA Foxconn. Ironically, Foxconn as well as other Acer suppliers, also build for HP!

ODM vs. OEM

The question is on the table: If an ODM that specializes in products (like a notebook PC) does everything for the OEM except the marketing function, at what point does the ODM take the last step and jump into the game, boosting those single digit margins to true OEM margins? Remember, the valuation of the largest EMS firms is in the gutter—most of which are trading at five- to ten-year lows.

The next logical step comes with a major *Core Competence* conflict. The CM provides a service to the OEM. In large, virtual factory/ODM arrangements, the CM does everything from design to ship, and even manages repairs and returns of the OEMs. But, to become an OEM may be to bite the hand that feeds it.

Presently, there are established, ready made distribution/sales channels, with large electronics super stores, such as Best Buy, Fryes, etc., as well as online shopping, like Tiger Direct. Additionally, as China and India continue their growth, internal needs create new markets for electronics and consumer goods. With this growth in demand and the pre-established retail distribution channels providing a tremendous "ease of entry," would it not make sense to offer a retail product (with significant margin) under your own brand?

> *May 01, 2007*
> *Asustek Computer will launch four Asus-branded low-cost notebooks with prices ranging from US$249–549 in July and begin to produce similar notebook-style PCs for Intel in September, the Chinese-language* Commercial Times *quoted company vice president Jerry Shen as saying. Shen made the remarks at an investors conference held on April 30, the paper noted.*
> *Unit sales of the low-cost notebooks, based on Intel's Classmate PC platform, are expected to total several hundred thousand to one million units in 2007 and top about 10 million in 2008, estimated Shen, who also noted that Asustek is likely to account for a 30–50% share of global sales of Intel-based low-cost notebooks projected for 2008.*
> *Source-DigiTimes*

Conflict arises and all of the OEM's questions immediately come into play:

> **Is this product being sold next to ours at the store for less money?**
> **Do they save the better (ODM) design for themselves?**
> **What happens to my schedule when there is increased demand for both products?**
> **Is my intellectual property being compromised?**

Can an OEM tolerate their CM being a competitor? Opinions on this will vary. If the CM's mission is to stay a CM, then they will tread very lightly.

> *Taiwanese Asustek Computer Inc., plans to split its operations of branding and EMS operations. The split was earlier planned to be done in 2008, however, the turbulence in the EMS-sector at the moment has pushed Asustek to proceed with the split as soon as possible.*

> . . . *Asustek plans to concentrate on branding business while creating a new EMS company. The Asustek move is aimed at challenging the status of Foxconn's No.1 position in the EMS sector.*

> *…Over the past few years, Asustek has seen mounting pressure from customers because of the conflict in the operations of branding and contract manufacturing, according to CENS.*
> *-Evertiq Jun14 2007*

The response from Asustek confirms a "tread lightly" approach. Making your largest customers uncomfortable about your business direction can prove disastrous, unless your direction is to leave the EMS sector in favor of a role as an OEM . . .

During a press conference announcing the of acquisition with Dopod International, Peter Chou, chief executive officer of High Tech Computer (HTC), stressed that the company will focus on own-brand business in the future.

> *When asking about the conflict between own-brand and OEM/ODM business, Chou reiterated the company's focus will be the own-brand sector and the orders from OEM/ODM will depend on market situation. He also highlighted the branding business will not hurt HTC's performance.*
> *- Irene Chen; Emily Chuang, Digitimes, May, 2007]*

What Sends it Away

Cost, plain and simple. It drives everything. Unless compelled to reduce costs, outsourced manufacturing and subcontracting would be done as close to home as possible, simple logic. It is the competitive nature of the world, the available world market, and the earnings per share of the OEMs that drive globalization. Are these sourcing strategies good decisions? Let's take a peek at the famous iPod. The following *teardown analysis* is an estimate of the content cost of one model:

80 GB version:

$ 110.00	Hard drive
$ 9.00	LCD screen
$ 8.50	Broadcom chip
$ 6.00	Lion battery
$ 5.80	SoC
$ 3.00	Wolfson Codec
$ 2.50	Click wheel
$ 9.00	Aluminum case

$153.80 total "A item" content. (Balance of material: $27.20)
$181.00 total material cost estimate on tear down.
 - *Apple Insider; Wedbush Morgan Securities*

Assuming a 7% markup on material, resulting in a 4–5% Gross Margin= $12.67

Can nearly $13 be saved by building it in house at an Apple factory? No. There are costs covered by the markup such as material freight, scrap, etc. But, the number looks like there could be about $10.00 of profit on material. The $181 of cost, plus $12.67 of markup, rounds to $194.00 for material and profit on material for the CM.

With a sell price of $349, that leaves a hefty $155 (44%) for value-add and profit (for Apple). And, let's remember that is retail. Wholesale pricing should land us around $290, leaving just a 33% margin ($96), not yet counting the labor costs to assemble it.

It is the value-add that sends it away (also some of the materials, like the housing is at an offshore price, being manufactured in Asia, but is listed in the material roll up).

Reports of $50/month wages make for sub $0.50 per hour direct labor rates. Even with a significant amount of overhead added to that, the resulting bid rates are miniscule when compared to the US. Some factories in China can be better described as a university setting, with dormitories, infirmaries, and complete food service and stores; the employees do not need to leave the property in the normal course of any given day. Even with these high overheads, fully burdened rates, including profit, can be sub $5 dollars per hour, compared to flat rates in the US of $30–$40 per hour for volume production.

If an iPod takes thirty minutes (guesstimate) to build, from kit drop to store ready packaging, the sourcing decision gets made for you. Even aggressively going with a $25/hr U.S. rate, there is 10 bucks to be made by making the product in Asia. More than 100 million iPods have been sold. That's a billion dollars in extra profit.

Of course it would take an insider to validate what is really going on with the iPod's cost and how the manufacturing agreement is structured, but the model suggests that the delta in costs is at least, if not larger than, that displayed above. And for every dollar better than the loose estimate above, that's one hundred million more to the bottom line.

While it makes financial sense to send the iPod to a low-cost region to be produced, is there not a sense of failure in doing so? Not that the good old USA is the only right place, nothing of that sort at all. But, if a company, say, in Spain, creates the next great gadget, and it needs to be built, would it not make sense to build it locally? The logistics and communications would be optimized, and the community in which it originates would benefit. Back in the day, towns were built up and created by the manufacturing of products. The automobile industry is probably the best example, but many smaller companies in many different industries have had a very large impact on their local communities. Today, we watch them vanish. Above is the reason why.

Another book to follow . . .

What Brings it Back

Mostly heard from our industry colleagues, are the other two things in the purchase equation: quality, and delivery/service.

These topics were most likely present in the decision to transition to the low-cost region, but were either undervalued, or miscalculated in the evaluation process, or the program is not what is was documented to be. Perhaps there were documentation issues that, along the learning curve with the former supplier, were remedied. This curve now starts over—on the other side of the planet, with a language barrier and 12-hour time difference, increasing the degree of difficulty.

> SHENZHEN, China—Universal Instruments (UI) has scrapped its manufacturing operation in Shenzhen, China, based upon persistent quality complaints from customers of its precision instruments.
> -Amy Wang, Contributing Editor—Electronic News, 8/16/2007

Product mix and dynamic demand can also kill an overseas manufacturing scenario. In addition to time zone differences for daily management, there is a freight lead time of 21 days (typical), where, once shipped, nothing can change. For Mexico, there are consolidated shipment issues to keep trucking freight costs in line. Once freight clears customs there is still lead time to get it to the dock. And don't forget a mid-winter, 3-week shut down for Chinese New Year (when dealing with China).

But, sometimes we want something (savings) so bad we will justify it in our minds. Let's look at a bad decision.

Real life:

An industrial controls manufacturer is looking to outsource their next generation product, which consists of a set of small printed circuit boards. CTI Technology, of Springfield, MA, has a local facility that is a very good match for their needs. The product will run in volumes estimated at 2500 per year. Once released, there is little chance of an engineering change, making this a steady production runner for the 30-man shop. During the discussion, CTI's Mexico fa-

cility is mentioned. The $7 per hour labor rate is exciting, but there is no fit, as the Mexico facility is 70,000 square feet and runs kit sizes at the customer's annual volume.

Yet, they keep coming back to it. The design stability and the steady demand will support a distant manufacturing scenario. But the volume is just too low. Ten minutes later, the conversation turns back: what about Mexico? Like pointing a baby sea turtle away from the ocean, no matter how many times the conversation returned to a local scenario, they spun back to Mexico and the $7 per hour rate. Finally, the president of the controls company insists on the Mexico facility and agrees to build all 2500 of each circuit card at once, and put them on his shelf.

Enter the purchasing manager. He is tasked with managing costs, delivery, and **inventory turns**. *As the Mexico facility processes the orders and readies for the builds, there is a request for a run of just 100. "No!" Then another conversation about a pilot run. "No!"*

Finally, a 100-piece qualification run is agreed to—followed by a build out of the 2400 unit balance—for each product. Then, the controls company needs additional product: another 200. They are supplying a couple of the components, and there appears to be some shortages on the balance of 2400, so can you run another 200?

The above program was doomed from the start. A bad fit was identified and it just got worse. Yet, companies will become blind to the issues when faced with a significant reduction in costs. The CM feared losing the deal and should have stood firm, knowing the decision was wrong. They missed an opportunity that would have been a good fit to build locally, at the proper cost.

Managing product returns can also be a nightmare. CTI Technologies held a manufacturing plant in Rosarito Mexico. A ceiling fan manufacturer discovers that many fans from a production run of fans were overheating. The issue was one component. Rather than send them back to China for an under warranty rework, they were sent, by the truck load to CTI for a $3 rework.

It is not likely that the fan manufacturer would reconsider its sourcing strategy, as these are low-cost, high volume products that fit the model, but this incident does highlight the risk and logistical challenges of managing an overseas product pipeline when there is a change in the demand or an issue.

Language barriers can also impact the success of a program. Even when the staff is trained in the language of the customer, there are often thick accents that make a normal conversation difficult to understand. Not only does it slow things down and make communications difficult, but also there is a sense of uncertainty that the information was received and understood in the right way. And sometimes it is not.

Imagine a three-way teleconference between the factory staff in Mainland China, a program manager from Down East Maine, and the customer in Scotland. Yikes!

When an overseas outsourcing effort does fail, the supply channel must stay intact to support market demand, while the issues are resolved. In a non-catastrophic event, this may result in a local source manufacturing a percentage of products to ensure availability during the evaluation and transition to a new strategic source. What has been seen by U.S. contract manufacturers (as described by a VP of business development at a tier one EMS provider), is a *boomerang to Mexico,* where manufacturing returns to North America, albeit, Mexico (this is most applicable to electronic assembly).

U.S.-based OEMs that are not satisfied with the results of the move to offshore manufacturing, must relocate production to another place. But, if it didn't work in China, why would it work in India or Thailand? But there is a significant internal problem the OEM must contend with. The purchasing agent/sourcing team lowered costs—and subsequently their standard costs in the cost of goods roll up in the ERP system—and went to press with the huge cost savings. This means that business models, including market sell prices, have been established considering the low overseas pricing.

These models must now be adjusted upward, diminishing profits or reducing market share due to a rise in the sell prices in order maintain the status quo on profits. To be the bearer of this news is not good for one's career at the OEM, especially if it was you who made the decision to go overseas in the first place. Thus, to lessen the blow, the OEMs tend to "stop off" in Mexico, before admitting defeat. There will be an increase in the TCO (Total Cost of Ownership), but a lesser blow to the bottom line.

Another risk to manufacturing offshore is the threat of **losing your intellectual property**. This is very real and has no apparent end in sight.

> *The incidents are the latest indications that cutting corners or producing fake goods is not just a legacy of China's initial rush toward the free market three decades ago but still woven into the fabric of the nation's thriving industrial economy. It is driven by entrepreneurs who are taking advantage of a weak legal system, lax regulations and a business culture where bribery and corruption are rampant.*
> *...*
> *"This is cut-throat market capitalism," said Wenran Jiang, a specialist in China who teaches at the University of Alberta.*
> *Counterfeiting, of course, is not new to China. Since this country's economic reforms began to take root in the 1980s, businesses have engineered countless ways to produce everything from fake car parts, cosmetics and brand name bags to counterfeit electrical cables and phony Viagra. Counterfeiting rings are broken nearly every week; nonetheless, the government seems to be waging a losing battle against the operations.*
> *-NYT*

Not only can your products be faked, but your intellectual property may become at risk when you move your manufacturing offshore or create the designs in an ODM relationship. This would result in a different product being on the market with your core design or technology residing inside. These products can be marketed in other regions without the OEM even knowing of their existence.

> *A company in the music industry invented an electronic guitar device that sells in considerable volume. The savings to manufacture the product in China allows them to offer a price point that will bolster sales and maintain a healthy profit. The actual specifications sent to China were intentionally incorrect, resulting in a nonfunctional product being manufactured—and passing a test as malfunctioning. Once the goods were received in the US, there was a simple rework process to undo the design flaws, then the product was deployed to the market. This secret rework was the company's way of protecting their IP and avoiding counterfeiting.*

At a lower level, counterfeit components are used to save cost. Your new Caller ID product may look like it has the Motorola processor driving it, but it may be a "bootleg" device, purchased at a fraction of the cost, with suspect performance and reliability.

Culture

Culture *(from the Latin cultura stemming from colere, meaning "to cultivate,") generally refers to patterns of human activity and the symbolic structures that give such activity significance. Different definitions of "culture" reflect different theoretical bases for understanding, or criteria for evaluating, human activity.*
  -Wikipedia

Culture is a touchy subject. If there is a comment made regarding a behavior of an ethnic group, or a country's people, there can be a backlash of criticism and claims of racism or prejudice against individuals, or the entire group. The fact is people are different: look around you. People come from different places on the planet and are, well, go ahead and say it, "different," including their behavior. This is called culture, isn't it? When culture is described in a negative way, it is unacceptable stereotyping.

> A program manager at SCI's Scotland facility dealt with many European accounts. When asked what it was like to do business in so many different countries, he said that each was very different. "Everyone does business in US dollars—that makes it easy. But the Germans—they negotiate you to four decimal places out, and it must be exact before anything happens. Grueling, yes, but there are no mistakes! Now the Italians—we hug, go to lunch and figure it out later. Everyone makes money! We love the Italians!"

This stereotyping comes from somewhere, from something. Also, there are traditions, such as large holidays like Chinese New Year and long shut down periods in Europe that define a country's industrial "personality." Cultural issues do impact manufacturing and must be considered when outsourcing in an international scenario.

There are commentaries, by those who do it for a living, that conducting business in the Far East can be difficult. Also, there are those who excel in international outsourcing and successfully maximize the benefits of doing business internationally.

Of maintaining business relationships in Asia, one consistent theme is heard: structure and task-driven responsiveness. A task is requested and a task is done. While this sounds optimal, when issues and problems arise that require problem solving, things come to a complete halt, often for many hours, while one side of the planet waits for the other side to wake up. This can be very frustrating, as no initiative was taken, nor is there any challenging of ideas, especially as you move down the organizational chart. People do not speak up; they just keep their heads down and do what's on the list, right or wrong. In the large factories of Asia, like the government, things are run in an authoritarian manner. The staff and employees listen well, then do exactly what was told.

To summarize the reports of colleagues who have launched products in Asia:

There is a huge gap in ability and savvy between the staff, the technicians, and the factory workers. The staffs of these facilities are highly educated executives. They may travel the world on business and interact with many cultures. They are also exposed to business models and practices, technical requirements and methods, etc. Down on the factory floor, however, there is a much different situation. Not that the factory floors elsewhere in the world have PhDs wandering around on them, but in the middle of the thousands of factory workers are the engineers and supervisory manufacturing staff trying to get the factory to build consistent product each day. It is these people, with engineer titles, who may not be what the customer expects them to be. No disrespect to the people here, as they are surely skilled, educated, and worked hard to achieve their position. But their given titles imply a different level of expertise, problem solving ability, and internal authority based on what they are called, when compared to the typical U.S. enterprise. The engineers and production floor staff at North American (and other) OEMs and CMs not only have responsibility for the manufacturing schedule and processes, but also the authority to make decisions and changes as required to ensure the objectives are met.

> **Real life:**
> China provides what we, and now Japan, cannot: an endless supply of cheap labor. The bid rates suggest $50 dollars a month wages. As stated by the quality manager of a large U.S. OEM making touch screens, the Asian manufacturing plant is an "ocean of humanity... Quality is achieved through continuous inspection." This comment was made in 1999. The director of materials for the same company said she could see the dormitories where the workers lived, but was not allowed to tour them.
>
> And, in 2002, when the owners of a $50 million Chinese EMS/ODM company were asked how they handled spikes in demand, they replied: "We send the bus up into the hills and it comes back full... They are ready in one week!"

These are the facts of the manufacturing culture in China. Other countries have stereotypes as well. Mexico has a reputation/stereotype for poor quality and an unreliable work force. In the early 2000s, wages in Mexico were about $1.50–$2.00 an hour. At $12–15 a day, the comparison is made to the panhandler washing windshields at the border crossing: they can make that in a day and be their own boss!

With industrial growth, the expendable, low-cost human resources also become mobile.

At CTI De Mexico, an 80,000 square foot EMS provider in Rosarito, Mexico, the work force was more stable than those companies 20 miles away in Tijuana. In Rosarito, there were only two electronics companies, CTI and Sharp Electronics. Employees could walk to work. Although Tijuana was an easy drive, the local facility offered those without vehicles opportunity for employment. To help ensure attendance, on site meals were subsidized, a family doctor was available 1–2 days a week, and bottled water was given to the employees. As far as compensation, a 15% bonus was given each week to any employee who showed up on time, every day.

These incentives helped, but when your competitive weapon is $15 a day wages, the weapon can be unreliable. In China there is at least a perception that the work force is more regimented, if not institutionalized. In either case, the warning, "you get what you pay for" is often a tough one to refute.

Other issues can arise for the manufacturer, as well. Although profiled above, it is not always as easy as sending the bus out to get employees when you need staff. An EMS/ODM with over 300,000 employees reported a 10% turnover in their work force annually. Most of this turnover occurs at the Chinese New Year holiday's three-week shutdown. Imagine coming off a three week shut down—needing to crank it out to the waiting customer base, and having 25,000+ people not show up for work!

The issues inherent to managing a mass of workers not returning from holiday will certainly create execution issues in the factory. This problem is exacerbated as China becomes more successful in manufacturing, as competitive factories create alternate employment opportunities for the workers. Mexico's industrialized cities, such as Tijuana, follow suit. When the wages are so low, and there is little to no benefit for longevity with a company, the workers have little reason to value job security, as there is no upside in the long term. A month's "vacation" may be in order, then, if the economy is good; a new job down the street at a competitor will suffice until enough is earned for another sabbatical or a trip home to the family in the hills of China.

The differences between individuals, people, and countries shape our planet. To deny they exist is foolish. To deny the rights of people to leverage these differences is criminal. We can all reflect more on this next winter, as we sit around our *holiday tree (courtesy of Mitt Romney)*.

Humanity

Recent news reports went back and forth the over the treatment of workers at the Foxconn factories that make iPods for Apple. Two factories came under the gun, with stories being stated, then retracted under threats of lawsuits.

The reality is that we want the products and we want to pay Walmart prices. Weather or not you agree with this, it is a *human behavior* and it is in line with pure capitalist theory. The iPod story is one that targeted a popular product, as are those stories about celebrity fashion designer clothing and the horrible factories that produce them. It seems it is news only if there is a popular name or item associated with it. The fact is, these conditions are more the norm than the exception.

Abuse Alleged at Disney Supplier

(HONG KONG)—Hundreds of people are making stuffed Walt Disney toys at a factory in southern China up to 16 hours a day with only a few days off a month, a Hong Kong-based labor activist group said Wednesday.
"During the peak season, before Christmas, workers at the factory start at 8 a.m. and don't finish until midnight," said Jenny Chan, an activist with the Hong Kong-based Students and Scholars Against Corporate Misbehavior.
Chan said the Tianyu Toys factory in the southern Chinese city of Dongguan regularly holds back workers' wages for up to 45 days, and paid overtime of 40 cents an hour, less than half the rate set by Chinese labor laws.
　　-AP, Nov., 2007

Not just in China, but around the globe there are many violations to the standards the US and many developed nations place on the treatment of people. It could be argued that our standards don't apply to certain places, where the standard of living is actually improving because of industrialization, even though it remains well below what we have come to expect as the minimum. While that argument is best left debated by those closer to the truth, the incredible demand for goods by the developed world will continue to create supply channels that will exploit the human and natural resources around them, and push the limits of the laws in whatever region they operate in, in order to win a chunk of the market and maximize profits.

The Environment

Manufacturing affects the environment in two ways. First, the products created will ultimately be thrown away. The materials in these products may be hazardous and non-biodegradable over time. Secondly, the factories pollute while making the products. Noxious fumes and materials are the byproducts of certain manufacturing processes, and significant energy is required to run the facilities. Some processes, such as the manufacturing of printed circuit boards, involve nasty chemicals to etch the traces in the copper and the application of toxic resins to create the layers.

Computing electronics has reshaped the planet—and redecorated it. With an obsolescence factor of just a few years, the turnover of the electronics is creating the "layer" of grey and beige plastic our descendents will dig through.

Recycling programs reclaim copper, gold, and other materials, along with some components, but the turnover of equipment has created a growing scrap pile that must now be addressed globally.

New environmental laws have emerged banning certain substances in Europe. The WEEE directive (Waste Electrical and Electronic Equipment) and the Restriction of Hazardous Substances (RoHS) Act were put into effect by the EC for all European countries in 2006. Other countries have adopted modified version of it as well.

The WEEE directive makes the manufacturers of electronics responsible for the ultimate removal of obsolete electronic goods from the European Community via recycling and or disposal.

RoHS bans substances such as lead and mercury from electronic products that are shipped to Europe. Fines are stiff, and products will be deported. An early warning shot was fired banning $100+ million in Sony gaming electronics for traces of cadmium in the device's wires. June 2006 was considered a *Y2K* event in the electronics industry, as RoHS took effect. For the most part, the EMS providers had to convert to a lead free solder in the manufacturing of printed circuit boards. As the clock wound down, there was widespread concern over the ability to comply.

The component suppliers had to convert to or offer lead free components. The identification of leaded vs. non leaded parts created a data management nightmare. Some parts were converted without changing the part number, requiring researching of the date codes for affectivity. As non-leaded parts were introduced, manufacturers rendered their leaded counterparts obsolete—creating more issues for OEM designs that were not converted to an RoHS compliant design.

The RoHS directive came with broad exemptions. For example: capital equipment, certain medical equipment, and server level telecom equipment are all exempt from the RoHS directive.

Before its implementation, the maneuvering started: a connector company claimed they could not guarantee the performance of their press fit connectors if they were RoHS compliant. Thus, a waiver was to be granted. But their direct competitor, TYCO, responded to the waiver by stating that they were compliant for two years in getting ready for the directive. An aircraft company politely refused to comply, as the lead free parts were yet not proven to be reliable and they would revisit the directive as long term reliability data became available. Furthermore, they stated, their airframes last for decades and are not tossed in the scrap heap every few years like the products targeted in the directive. It seems the directive's exemptions would not jeopardize our ability to surf the 'Net, but would take a leap of faith in the sky! These examples were posted on the EC's website during the "readiness" period in 2005.

It appears the lead free parts do have issues. "Tin whiskers" may appear on circuit boards. These metal threads "grow" out of a solder joint potentially shorting out the component to whatever it touches.

At a 2006 trade show in Boston, a company was displaying its capability to re-lead parts for reliability and mil spec compliance. They underscored a recent space shuttle delay resulted from an "unleaded" tin whisker creating a short, taking down onboard electronics.

All of this brings about some chaos—and opportunity. New companies formed overnight in the quest for compliance. Much like the ISO 9000 and the *Sarbanes-Oxley* crazes, consultancy companies appeared everywhere to assist in the need to be "green."

> *5-Trees, of Burlington, MA, was formed specifically to address the RoHS directive. Their focus is in education, training, and compliance analysis for OEM companies.*

Manufacturing presents the other environmental impact. The very process to create these toss-able products is not clean. Period. Not only are the processes themselves unclean, but the factories that house the processes, the packaging materials for components, etc., can all be considered a target for waste and emission reduction.

Plating and painting metal parts, plastics molding, PCB fabrication, lead soldering, leather tanning, etc., all result in environmentally-unfriendly waste and emissions. Regulations create a new kind of motivation. Profit-seeking companies not only gravitate to where labor is cheap, but to where a lack of regulations, or lack of their enforcement, can enhance profits. In this global economy there are many places one can go where toxic byproducts can be dumped right into the environment without processing, thus creating a lower purchase price for the consumer.

China is in the middle of an industrial revolution. This revolution is not clean, as a large percentage of the world's raw materials, such as concrete and aluminum, are manufactured there. Additionally, coal is abundant and powers the majority of factories, creating air pollution. Over 300,000 premature deaths are attributed to the air quality annually, reports *The New York Times*. In the same article the World Bank estimates that 750,000 people die form pollution annually (air and water.) In another article, the *Times* states that one-third of China's carbon emissions come from the manufacturing of products that are exported.

> *"... the outside world is a partner in degrading the country's environment. Chinese manufacturers that dump waste into rivers or pump smoke into the sky make the cheap products that fill stores in the United States and Europe..."*
> -NYT, Aug 2007

This excuse for China's out of control pollution issues seems preposterous. Yet, we, as a society, endorse and promote it, with an *out of site, out of mind* mentality. As long as we can buy more stuff and buy it cheaper, we don't mind that people die of lead poisoning, or from lung diseases from air laden with coal soot. Nor do we mind water pollution that is so bad that marine life cannot be sustained. That is, until it hits *our* back yard. The reality is that part of the reason countries, such as the US, have cleaner air is because they now get their products such as steel, concrete, and printed circuit boards from China rather than having a dirty factories on their own land.

So, we point overseas and tell them they are ruining the planet and to clean it up . . . while watching the news report on our new, imported plasma screen TV and then e-mailing our congressman on our laptop from Shenzhen—all gotten at unbelievable prices!

And oh, by the way, at the time of this writing the good 'ole USA was still number one at emitting greenhouse gases.

Economic Swings
What a difference a few months make!

The current economic crisis is certainly taking its toll on the contract manufacturing industry. This downward swing is not a one time event, however. But, when speaking about the present geopolitical and economic situation, it is very clear that we have never been here before. The stock market has been this low, but not off of such a high. The lending institutions are flirting with disaster. There is a new president. There are two wars. And there is a trillion plus dollars being spent by the government to stop the bleeding. Interesting times ahead!

If we look back at the electronics boom's short history, there have been swings worthy of note. Just as things were booming, the semiconductor/capital equipment industry fell flat on its face in 1998. The wave ripped thorough their "value chain."

> *Wire Techniques LTD, a small cable assembler in Chelmsford, Mass, employed about 40 people. Their largest customer was PRI Automation, a capital equipment manufacturer for the semiconductor industry. The OEM would fax orders daily, declaring the lengths of the cables needed for each system install; the orders would be built and shipped within a two week lead time. One day, no orders came over the fax. None the next, and so on... Eighteen workers were laid off over the next few weeks.*

The economic impact was not so widespread, as it was more industry specific. And, as the industry recovered, eyes looked East. Outsourcing overseas was in high gear. The job shops were suffering badly as machined parts, cable assemblies, monitors, etc., all could be obtained at a significant savings.

Then, in 2001, the other shoe fell...

The train wreck came with the implosion of the dot coms and the telecom market. Many of the job shops and CMs were already licking their wounds from the rising craze to take *the good* business to the Far East.

Small machined parts were becoming a commodity, being brokered offshore. Metal fabrication and stampings were also seeing significant cost reductions when moved to Asia and India. The EMS industry was now mature enough to confidently, albeit, cautiously, move production of higher volume, stable products overseas. It was a knockout blow for some.

It seemed that orders vanished overnight. The dot coms were vanishing too and the orders from the telecoms were pushed out. Any work in progress (WIP) or finished goods was worthless unless paid for by telecom. The component distributors, at the bottom of food chain, bricked up their docks to stop the material returns. Many small telecoms tanked without paying their bills. What was left was a huge surplus of material and capacity. The contract manufacturers dropped prices to the point of just trying to keep their machines fed, quoting business at prices that would only allow them to break even, sometimes even taking a loss, just to absorb overhead. As shops closed, equipment was auctioned off, tanking the capital equipment market. The stock market plummeted.

The recovery from these events is never pretty. The survivors are typically the shops that had been in business a long time and could ride out the storm *(read: low or no debt, lots of cash)*. Some survivors picked up business from those who did not make it. Others consolidated, as *bottom feeding* can provide opportunities.

Wire Techniques, LTD, profiled in a previous example, was a survivor, having been in the business for 20 plus years. As things sort themselves out, a nearby CM fell and WTL picked up a new customer and a few employees.

Time heals the wounds: a year of slow business, perhaps even a posted loss, then, steady recovery. As the market sorted itself out, nature took its course, and **thinned the herd**. Doors closed and quick sell offs occurred in the eleventh hour, avoiding an ugly chapter 11 or 7 filing.

Like seagulls at the dump, CMs went after any piece of business they could grab. Their core competence pitch changed like the wind: "We are a low volume house, a high volume house, a-whatever-you-got house ..."

In a "getting back to business" mode, a **backlash** starts. The component suppliers reel first. They watched the dust settle, holding the bag on inventory and receivables from OEMs and CMs. Now, they are calling the shots. Terms become tighter. And now "who you are" will dictate what price you get. The manufacturers weren't completely out of trouble, and price and terms would be adjusted depending on risk and how their business was handled during the "ugly" period. For some troubled EMS providers, terms were difficult to establish, and it is these terms which are integral to cash flow (as we will see later on).

The CMs followed suit and became more conservative. They went back to their original business model. They pushed back, some demanding cash in advance. After all, they survived when other CMs, as well as OEMs, didn't—sticking them with the bill. Those still barely hanging on remain aggressive looking at any and all types of opportunities—and it quickly becomes obvious who they are.

In the **short term**, the "astute" purchasing agent at the OEM may take advantage of this opportunity to lower purchase prices and create favorable cost variances, called **Purchase Price Variance**, or PPV, where the standard cost (i.e., book price) of an item is now higher than the actual price, resulting in additional profits. But transitioning to that new supplier comes with cost and risk. Many OEMs now look at a Total Cost of Ownership model (TCO) in an attempt to capture transition and logistics costs. But in some companies, the purchasing agent may have an incentive riding on achieving a PPV number. The personal objective placed on the purchasing agent may in fact, create behavior not in the best interest of the company, as the supplier's low ball quote may just be foreshadowing of the inevitable. Product deliveries may suffer if the supplier has credit issues with their raw materials' suppliers. Also, one must assume that the struggling supplier's staff is kept to a minimum to keep the doors open, so overall service will suffer. But, the purchasing agent has posted a favorable variance vs. the previous prices and has done his or her job (read: "Bonus!").

The final dagger is when the cash-strapped CM factors, or sells their invoices. Very few recover from this tactic. "Factoring" is to ship a product, bill the customer, then "sell" the invoice to another financial entity and receive cash immediately. The customer is notified that the receivable is now due to the other entity. The CM does this to create quick cash flow needed to sustain the operation. The financial company provides that, by "buying the outstanding invoice"—albeit at a discount, say, 90%–95% of the invoice. The CM has just given away their precious thin margin in order to make payroll or buy more parts to keep the lines running. Without some other form of cash, there is little hope to recover from this death spiral. The customer is the first to know, having to now pay a third party. Then the supply chain, who already knew they had cash issues, resorts to (if they haven't already) COD or CIA (Cash in Advance). The fat lady starts singing . . .

Collateral Damage

As mentioned earlier, the train wreck's **other victim** was the equipment manufacturers. Not only did they watch their customers slow down, but those that failed created a huge inventory pool of used (some barely used) equipment for the survivors. As the market recovered, the equipment sales folks sat on the sidelines, waiting for this inventory to be consumed. This event can take a complete sales cycle out of the equipment industry, as they must wait for the "near new" equipment to go obsolete before the next sale can be made.

In the **long term,** the weak and leveraged fell as the industry sorted itself out; the recovery revealed a new personality to the industry. Telecom was a bad word, but the OEMs still had the buyer's market mentality. Their problem was that the stick they carried had shrunk. In addition to a tarnished reputation, schedule commitments were now kept as low as possible; lead times and ordering terms were negotiated as much as pricing. The CMs were not about to negotiate, and the distributors stood firm on their payment terms. The sharing of cost data all but vanished. This did not deter the OEMs, as there was still a surplus of capacity.

They looked east again. The doors were open.

As the utilization and revenue numbers gradually returned to normal, the push for offshore manufacturing left a gaping hole in the U.S. factories. Although the growth numbers were back to 20% annually, and the economy was strong—the stock market booming—the industry was still adjusting, and the top tier of EMS companies was showing little or no profit. But Foxconn continued to stretch its lead.

Contract electronics manufacturer Jabil Circuit Inc. . . . reported an 80 percent drop in quarterly earnings on Thursday because of

> *higher costs, including restructuring charges and stock-based compensation.*
> *Reuters, May, 2007*

Smaller CMs shifted their marketing strategies to military, medical, and industrial controls. Certifications were the investment in the future, while the larger shops adjusted their footprint to accommodate the emerging regions of Eastern Europe, Vietnam, and India. This new development was to accommodate the new demand for hand-held computing and communicating.

This is the tidal flow of the contract manufacturing market. It is happening again—and it is a moon tide. This time it has hit all industries, as well as the lending institutions. The shake out will be huge; some companies have already fallen.

> *ACT Manufacturing files Chapter 11 in 2002, a dot bomb casualty. ACT Electronics emerged after an asset purchase of the remains, only to file Chapter 7 (liquidation) in October of 2008. Their Mississippi facility was sold, just prior, to Ayreshire Electronics, as the customer base was solid enough to interest Ayreshire.*

As the economy tightened in 2008, the EMS companies reacted, closing facilities and halting some expansion in emerging countries. Eastern Europe has seen a lot of pull back as has Vietnam, EMS companies now seeing large scale development in emerging countries as a risk as global demand for products falls.

Even Foxconn slowed investment, but in July of 2008, Evertiq reported a 35% growth from the previous year, on track to their projected growth numbers. It looked as though, while they would be impacted, Foxconn was running away from the pack, with a huge share of the consumer electronics market.

Finally, in December, Evertiq reported that Foxconn would lay off 100,000 employees "in preparation for the financial crisis."

As we watch the new president work various bailout plans, no one knows where this will go. But, if you study the happenings over the last ten years, you can predict certain things that will happen over time.

Companies will fall. Maybe even one or two big ones, although a merger is more likely as a preemptive move. The big dogs have all taken "goodwill" write downs, wiping out any 2008 profits in preparation for 2009, Flextronics taking the largest, at $5.8 billion. They have all also reset revenue objectives and announced layoffs in the thousands, along with the aforementioned facility closings.

Perhaps the acquisition of Solectron will prove to be badly timed, if the recovery is slow in coming and they cannot fuel the factories acquired that support a more high tech, telecom market. And for many, the ability to finance those huge blocks of inventory may become a thing of the past.

And the mighty Foxconn has warned their market of lower profits, though they have not halted investment in a multi-billion dollar complex in Vietnam to provide lower labor rates amidst the rising rates China is experiencing.

Some or all of the answers may be clear by the time you're reading this. What we do know from the present data is that the industry will adapt and recover, leaving the strong intact to adjust to the next chapter in this relatively short story.

Summation

We define contract manufacturing as any service to a firm that creates or advances the creation of that firm's products or sublevel components. Recognizing that this business is a service, marketing departments pitch a model of core competence in manufacturing processes, materials management, and capacity balancing—something often difficult for an OEM. Thus, the CM's profits are determined by doing the job as, or better than, planned, including: purchasing raw materials, building the products, and quality yields.

The EMS sector (the largest, by far) has drastically changed over the last ten years, morphed by the world's skyrocketing demands for electronics, which has reshaped the way the world does business.

In the short history of this revolution there have been significant highs and lows in the contract manufacturing market space and its supporting capital equipment market. The recoveries happen, but not without casualties in this continuously growing, yet volatile market. The manufacturing zone is now the world, as technology and logistics have enabled enterprises to manufacture and market their products in almost any region of the planet at the lowest available cost.

Recently, more available services have been added to the EMS's offerings, working toward the vertical integration model that they originally broke, introducing the ODM model—one very short step from being an OEM.

As the smaller CMs lose the "gravy" to the low-cost, offshore manufacturers, they retreat to the business profile that started them back when the OEMs did production in house: providing a local capability with high service for prototypes, short runs, and emergency buys. The remaining domestic market also includes medical products and military work, and CMs are acknowledging this by investing in the certifications necessary to perform these manufacturing services.

And now, all CMs must embrace the new environmental regulations that were spawned in Europe and are gradually being accepted and adopted worldwide.

Today, the price of oil is impacting logistics. The dollar is weak. And in Q4 of 2008, the world got flipped upside down by the financial markets. What toll will this take on the $50 billion of domestic business to the small to medium contract manufacturers? And will this cause us to rethink the way we manufacture globally? These global players have their backs to the wall, having run ultra thin margins (sub 5%) for the last five years attempting to capture the new demands of consumer and handheld electronics.

Another shakeout is certainly upon us in the years to come, but with the world economy, banking crisis, and possible demise of the automotive industry as we know it, predicting the next five to ten years requires a very large crystal ball.

5. Philosophical DNA

The Dilemma

There is a perception in the manufacturing industry that contract manufacturing companies, specifically EMS providers, are "cheap." The pay is less than a comparable job at an OEM, the benefits are not as good, and the burnout rate is higher because the staff is kept to a minimum. Also, equipment additions and staffing increases to support growth appear to be handled in an *almost in time* manner, rarely putting capacity in front of demand, resulting in the shop floor always playing catch-up during the "good times."

Bingo! This is how the money is made.

At SCI, program managers made (in the '90s) the equivalent wages of an OEM's buyer (not senior buyer). The roles and responsibilities of the two were different with regard to the expectations of the individual.

A buyer must have basic knowledge of the commodities he or she is procuring, must be able to interpret an MRP/ERP, and have a decent understanding of best practices in purchasing, inventory management, and quality, in addition to being tasked with goals and objectives on PPV (Purchase Price Variance) and on-time delivery. For buyer positions, it is preferred that candidates have 1–3 years experience and a college degree.

The program manager at the CM is responsible for the business in its entirety. He or she would negotiate the contract for his/her customers, execute the proposal (with input from materials and engineering), establish the cost standards in the ERP, then reconcile the actuals and report the P&L for the business segments managed. Additionally, he or she presents at business reviews both internally and with the customer. On a daily basis, the program manager is the primary point of contact for the customer's wants and needs, along with the higher level, "fun" stuff. Program manager positions require an engineering or business degree, plus 3–5 years experience.

*In addition to the workload and pay issues, SCI kept costs in line throughout the organization. The phone systems were out of date—no voice mail (when everyone else had it)—program administrators and production planners shared a PC in their shared cubicles, and the ERP was considered "vintage," with fuzzy green monitors. At one SCI facility, the marketing manager's expense report was bounced for listing a **refill** for his Cross pen. "Get a Bic!" he was told. Thrifty indeed!*

This behavior lives on. How else can a company with no product to offer, no market exclusivity, and a level paying field of competitors win business and be successful?

When joined together in a business relationship, the contract manufacturing company and the OEM create a dilemma. If the decision is made to outsource a manufacturing process presently done in house, the OEM's internal manufacturing staff must be let go. Shutting down an internal manufacturing process is not a simple transaction or transition. There will be mixed emotions from the internal staff; jobs are being lost. For those remaining, control is lost—and so is pride. This translates to a sensitive relationship out of the gate with the new manufacturing partner.

Furthermore, the OEM has come to the CM for what they could not provide: efficient manufacturing of their products. The CM has taken over, and must now service the OEM and satisfy them (is that possible?), all at a lower, fixed price. Providing this service, by design, is a much leaner operation than the customer had (in terms of a domestic divestiture).

Often, the result is a well staffed, well qualified team, watching a lesser staffed, lower paid team performing their previous job duties. This often creates conflict and criticism from the team letting go. After all, how can a lowly contract manufacturer replace a highly trained, *world-class* OEM staff such as Motorola's, when the new staff does not have the credentials or the industry expertise that the original staff possesses? Additionally, a company like Motorola has such a presence in the industry that the CM's supply chain could never be as responsive or price competitive (*Just why* were *they outsourcing?*).

Therefore, in a divestiture of manufacturing, human behavior (HBO) at the OEM can push for the CM to fail—in order to prove they did not.

> *Kodak /EPPS, a prepress solutions company, elected to outsource their manufacturing to SCI. The SCI team visited EPPS and was to review their processes and start the transition. As the team was given the factory tour, the workers walked out, leaving a designee at each work center to "stare down" the team.*

While the underlying desire to have the CM fail may not always be present, the OEM can easily out-staff the team at the CM. Some OEMs are designed from day one to outsource the majority or all of their manufacturing. In start up mode, the OEM has a small team—maybe one person. Then, as more products are designed, the organization grows, and the emphasis on supply chain management becomes paramount, as the largest piece of COGS (Cost of Goods Sold) is the purchase orders to the EMS provider. And when the going gets tough, the CM can easily be overwhelmed by the customer. The OEM's staff is focused only on their products, while the CM's staff may have multiple customers to handle, unless the account is of a very large magnitude.

Here again, the relationship is structured to invite conflict. The CM's purchasing staff is managing the materials to satisfy many products being built for many customers. The OEM's staff is larger, and only focused at the product level, or key components in their products. When issues occur, regardless of their origin, the opportunity presents itself to demonstrate they are the experts and show the CM how it's done. The specialist at the CM, on the other hand, may be perfectly capable (*or not*) to handle this, but just does not have the bandwidth to be responsive. Thus, while they welcome the help, they don't appreciate the lecture that often comes with it.

> ***Real life example:***
> *As the telecom bubble reached it maximum diameter, times were nothing less than chaotic. Just as one telecom IPO'd, they transferred manufacturing from one CM to another in a panic, because the incumbent could not support their exploding needs.*
>
> *Along with the new customer and revenue, came a materials manager that voted "No" to the transition—and made it very clear. Also, materials inaccuracies from incumbent EMS provider's inventory transfer caused production issues as well as a strategic third party distributor not making commitments. Amidst the chaos and finger pointing, secret after hour meetings were held at the EMS provider by different factions from the OEM—positioning themselves for their next round of internal meetings. The politics were so severe that two lawsuits were known about with regard to discrimination and compensation. There was also the constant flow of staffing additions to support the growth—the new adds constantly comparing their potential net worth to the previous stock option packages that were handed out.*
>
> *When all was said and done, and every unit scheduled had been shipped, and all revenue goals met or exceeded. The QBR (Quarterly Business Review) that followed had everyone in attendance. The OEM's (new) materials manager notified the EMS provider's CEO that they did not appreciate the "diving catch" the EMS provider made to save their year end—and they better sharpen up, or be replaced as a supplier.*

Fortunately, the EMS provider's team carried no weapons. While they felt they had done a good deed—the one the other EMS provider (top 3, by the way) could not do—they forgot they were dealing with personal agendas, and not a corporate mission.

Business Methodology

For the most part, contract manufacturing is a "reactive" business. Nearly everything a CM does is in reaction to a customer purchase order or formal change order.

Capacity is rarely placed in front of demand. There may be some strategic moves made based on a business forecast, but you don't go out and buy an additional surface mount line ($1 mil) or Amada Punch Press ($300K) without the need for it. In a growing CM, this means they are playing "catch-up." Demand has outweighed capacity and incremental additions are being made to support the growth, which has been determined <u>not</u> to be a one time spike. *The watchful eye is right on plan . . .*

So, with any CM in growth mode, it is a safe bet that they are having trouble meeting their customers' delivery requirements. These are good times for a CM as a business, but not necessarily for the employees. While the machines are maxed out, so is the staff, working OT and weekends. The employees become cooked from the daily grind of the customers' need to know detailed schedules, now that product is late. And, only as it becomes painfully obvious that an area is understaffed, or needs equipment, do approvals to add get granted. The daily scramble sees material shortages and scheduling conflicts exacerbating the problems. But the utilization is through the roof! And the revenue line is climbing . . . *The boss in on cloud 9*. This is how most CMs manage growth.

6. Competence

Contract manufacturers, while in different service offerings, share the same basic core competence needs. Service administration, materials, and manufacturing process control may vary, depending on the type of business the CM is in, but the need for consistent execution and proper asset management is the common foundation for these competencies. For example, metal shops will have less complex materials planning than an EMS company, but the core ability to source and manage materials is shared. Engineering/technical skills will, of course, differ widely from industry to industry.

Service / Contract Administration

First and foremost, the customer needs a point of contact to route all business and communications through. In small CMs there may be a customer service manager handling all business. As shops get larger, there is segregation of tasks and customer "teams" emerge, with representatives from various disciplines including materials, planning, quality, and engineering. In large EMS companies, these teams may be dedicated to a specific customer—if the revenues are large enough to warrant it.

Typically, the **program manager** is the team leader and owner of all formal communication with the customer. This is the person who receives requests, purchase orders and change requests, then responds with commitments to the customer. All business issues including schedules, quality issues, costing and administrative issues typically fall under this role. In larger companies, program managers have a certain amount of responsibility for the success of the customer account and may even report the P&L. They are also the ones standing up front at your business reviews.

In larger CMs, the primary rule that must be respected is, "If he or she didn't commit it, don't count on it." If a change to the specification is handed from the OEM's engineer to the CM's engineer, there is a great risk to its successful implementation. If there is a team leader on the OEM's side, all business critical requirements flow through that Point of Contact (POC), on through to the program manager. Additionally, any schedule or ordering issues also need to go through the proper channels.

> *Scenario:*
> Customer "A's" quality manager walks into their CM and corners the operations manager, stressing the need for delivery he just heard about in a meeting. The ops manager says, "Can do!" While this is happening, the president of the company and his program manager are on the phone with Customer "B," ensuring they will drop everything and get their product out this week.
>
> The next day, Customer "A" has a meeting and the quality manager provides the schedule information he got while on site. You can see where this is going.

Service (and Responsiveness) is championed by the program manager, because it often provides a looking glass into how well a company performs. Often, their job boils down to managing expectations, perceptions, and information. As things get hectic, there is a need for a sense of order: who controls the information on what is going to happen and when, not only in the manufacturing of products, but the actual exchange of the information itself.

Another business aspect the program manager is responsible for is **Contract Administration,** and it is often very underrated. Here is why:

Contract manufacturers create things that are pretty much useless to anyone but the customer who ordered them. Once the raw materials have labor/value added, there is a 100% risk factor, until the customer pays the bill. Risks and liabilities are typically defined with formal contracts (in addition to purchase order coverage, AKA "releases") that outline the rules of engagement, financial obligations, scheduling and rescheduling rules, product warranty, as well as disengagement.

If there is no contract, the purchase order is typically considered the governing body. More often than not, there is a lack of documentation on the rules of the relationship between manufacturer and OEM, and the purchase order Terms & Conditions can be a bit generic, having lengthy legal statements, but nothing addressing the specific order. The sequence of events often occurs this way:

1. There is a RFQ (Request for Quotation) from the OEM to the CM. This is often a standard form with the OEM's *Terms and Conditions* for doing business.

2. The CM replies with a response with their *Terms and Conditions* for doing business on it.

3. The OEM then releases a purchase order to the CM, which again, has their *Terms and Conditions* on it.

When something goes wrong, the CM could argue that the OEM accepted their quote and the OEM could argue that they accepted their purchase order. This is just a bad job done by both parties. In the business relationship the CMs are "order hungry" and the OEMs need product. The details are often overlooked, an, by the time they need to be understood, it's often too late.

The need for a contract or manufacturing agreement grows proportionately with the size and complexity of the business to be awarded. When risks grow, the impact is larger when things go wrong.

Traditional mindset is a simple action/reaction behavior. OEM places purchase order. CM starts buying materials and scheduling factory. No forecast, no schedule sharing, no pull systems, no Kan Ban, nothing—until a purchase order (typically non-cancelable) is on the books.

It is the contract manufacturing company's MRP system that then causes the "reaction." When the order is entered, the MRP drives the factory to start buying parts and planning capacity for the "work order" to be built. And, with the EMS industry, odds are, there are at least a handful of parts whose lead time and/or stock situation will not support the schedule entered into the MRP.

Even though the OEM may share the forecast with the CM, nothing (transactional) typically happens until the purchase order is placed. The forecast is a nice panning tool—for discussion only. Anyone in the downstream supply chain aligning inventory or capacity to support the forecast, does so at their own risk.

Of course there are exceptions. You can bet that in the world of iPod manufacturing, there are much more sophisticated forecasting and scheduling systems, replete with EDI (Electronic Data Exchange) links, scenario analysis, and state of the art supply chain replenishment programs. But we are talking about two massive factories, 25,000 workers making a handful of similar little products made in the millions, and one customer! For the rest of us in the manufacturing world, it's not so glamorous.

Prepare for the lawsuit. You wear a seat belt, right? Documenting the $@#^! out of everything is not a bad idea. Over the long term, you will be better off for it. Odds are you won't end up in court, but throughout the relationship you will be considered the expert, not be challenged, and be in control of the relationship. The job mandates it, yet, it is often the last priority.

Additionally, a proper contract will define the rules, at least initially. Flexibility and responsiveness are key competences a CM should have, and the contract's section on scheduling and rescheduling will at least set the baseline expectations of the customer and minimum requirements for the CM (Recall Barbosa's reply to the request to honor the Pirates' Code in the movie *Pirates of the Caribbean*: "They're really more like guidelines...").

Real life example:
A small CM engages with a very small engineering company that has a new product they believe will take off. It is a complex box build involving 2 PCBs, 7 cable assemblies, box level assembly and two functional tests...

All is great; the two agree to do business and make the first 500 units of a 1500 unit forecast. The first 500 are made as the final processes, including test, are defined.

The customer then releases 100 units, with a 30-day lead time. This delivery must be hit, at all costs. Well, at all costs to the CM, anyway. Initially, the project was costed at releases of 500 units with a 6–8 week lead time. The price for some items is more than double in the lower volume. The customer needs product, but the CM cannot honor the negotiated price at the lower volume. The customer insists the 1500 will be ordered by their customer and doesn't understand what the problem is. A week later, the customer releases another 200—a surprise order from their end customer. "See, we told you!" Of course, the 200 were requested for the same delivery as the initial order, after the CM had to reset everything in play to support the first release!

In the above scenario, all are to blame for any stress or misunderstanding. The good news here is that the business materialized and there were no bad intentions from either party. The contract manufacturer was actually building the cable assemblies in advance of the release, in an attempt to improve the lead time. In a downside situation, this would get very ugly, very fast. To step back and properly document some rules and responsibilities would make the relationship more comfortable and the order easier to execute.

Let's look at the lead time. The end customer wanted 30 days, so the engineering firm agreed. The CM did not. This is a condition of doing business with the end customer, so it must happen. The bare circuit boards have a 3–4 week lead time alone, not counting manufacturing time, which has over 3 hours per assembly. So, if we just don't talk about it, 30 days it will be. The orders come in and the CM commits to

6 weeks, and the customer says, "You know we need them in 30 days." The customer later beats the CM up for being late. This behavior is prevalent throughout the industry. The CM fears their competition will say *"Yes! Can do!"* even though they would have the same challenges. But they would have the order. So, it may be best to dance around the issue, get the order, and disappoint a little.

A simple contract that documented minimum purchase quantities and an advance purchase of the boards, as well as defining liability on the CM building ahead on the cable assemblies would make everyone's life a bit easier—and probably get to a 30-day lead time.

Change Management

Combining the processes and the people in charge of execution, change management will be only as good as the staff that enforces its rules.

Contract manufacturers receive data in variable formats from multiple customers and formalize it into a common format for processing. When change occurs, the change notice (internal document) is routed throughout the enterprise and has an *impact analysis* done by all applicable disciplines. The "impact" can entail: billable rework for work in progress, modifications to test equipment and other tooling, cost and lead time changes resultant from new components, billable obsolete inventory for components removed, or, billable scrap. A formal response is routed back to the customer and the changes (and charges) are approved, or disapproved. This must be a firm and rigid process, one where the flexibility demands of the customer must be kept in check, even at the expense of responsiveness. (For an OEM looking to outsource, this is an excellent place to audit during your due diligence.)

In addition to being a critical path item to risk management, change management is critical to manufacturing execution, which flows down to efficiency and profitability. Changes not only to configuration, but also to schedule must be efficiently analyzed and implemented. Shifts in product delivery schedules resulting in the rescheduling of the supply chain is also an integral part of change management and is covered in more detail below.

Manufacturing / Process Control

The key competence of the Manufacturing Department at the CM is **process control.** Multiple customers means multiple products, multiple documentation formats, and different lot sizes, all running through one common, controlled environment. The contract manufacturer must be able to demonstrate (up front) that their processes have controls that will take varying specifications of varying products in varying lot sizes and simultaneously produce a mixed bag of products, exactly to their specifications and volumes, in a repeatable, ongoing manner.

> *Real life:*
> Riverside Precision Sheet Metal, Henniker, NH, 12+/- people, $2+ million annually.
>
> Riverside will first produce 50 front panels for an EMS company; the end customer is Raytheon, the job thus requiring military certifications, serialization, cage code, and lot code traceability.
>
> The next job to the line: 500, 3-foot-long scissors, used for ribbon cutting ceremonies, sketched by their engineer Keith, and the customer said, "Swell, do it!"
>
> Third up: 2 pieces of a bracket for a telecom start up, from an emailed CAD drawing marked HOT: "Need in three days, no paint. PO to follow. Let me know how much."
>
> Fourth up: 10 Ford Taurus grill templates for a NASCAR team. No drawings, no charge (the owner is on the pit crew.)

Process control must standardize the variables coming through the front (and back) door, and process them in a like manner through the various work centers. At the EMS provider, new documentation is often created, standardizing what the factory floor sees, and internal revision controls can be employed to manage change control. The sheet metal shop, on the other hand, may take the customer blueprint (drawing) and have it attached to the shop floor work instructions, or "traveler."

Process control goes beyond the manufacturing floor. Order/change order management, configuration management, manufacturing engineering (process documentation), material control, etc., all will affect the manufacturing process if they drift out of control.

A Quality Plan or ISO documentation will outline the procedures and how they are maintained. Also, if there are DOD contracts or FDA, FAA, UL, CSA or other agency approved contracts being administered in the factory, files, plans and audit results will be maintained.

Layout, as stated earlier, becomes very similar in large shops. The processes to manufacture are the same for each competitor in a given service offering, thus the shop floor of each factory will flow the same, albeit some better than others. And, physical constraints of the facility may disrupt the flow of processes. For example, if a company is located in a large, old mill building, they may share a receiving and shipping dock—far from where the material flow would otherwise designate the locations.

Receiving Dock → Incoming Inspection → Stock Room → Kitting/Prep → Manufacturing → Test/Inspection → Shipping Dock

The above flow, if laid out optimally, would make a factory look like a car wash. Yet, many factories don't look this way for many reasons. Primarily, the physical space many factories occupy was preconfigured with offices, manufacturing space, and the docks, as fixed locations prior to the layout being defined. Also multiple functions may be handled by the same people, such as "shipping and receiving," thus requiring a U-shaped flow where the finished product exits the building where the raw materials enter it. This is a very common set-up in small, as well as some very large, manufacturing companies. Due to physical constraints of the facility, material and work in progress may travel up and down levels and long distances for certain operations requiring special physical needs, such as ventilation, clean rooms, or the need to be far from others, like painting.

> *Grain Surfboards, of York, Maine, manufactures wooden surfboards. While they are an OEM, they build their surfboards to order, in lot sizes of one. In fact, the "assembler" travels through the process with the board, performing all manufacturing processes. These boards are considered art, and the builder signs his or her work. The final processes involve epoxy and sanding; the two work centers are located in a loft above the rest of the operation. Epoxy and sanding are at opposite ends of the work environment; one is delicately brushing glue over crafted wood and the other violently sending dust into the air. It would be best to have these two processes as far apart from one another as possible. But, the boards receive many coats of epoxy, and are sanded between each coat after sitting to cure/dry. It was decided—for efficiency—to locate the two next to each other and reduce the repeated travel of the Work in Progress. Also, the cure time needed, placed the WIP out of the way of the other processes. With the movement of product optimized, the issue was to not contaminate the epoxy area with dust, as well as proper ventilation for worker safety.*

The formal monitoring of **cycle times** also demonstrates competence in the manufacturing process and is regularly benchmarked by customers. The quest for reduction in cycle times also demonstrates a policy of "continuous improvement." While the model you have may be winning business (therefore, its good, if profitable), customers look for shorter production cycle times to lower their liability and increase schedule flexibility. Cycle time reduction in larger factories, especially the EMS providers, is talked about daily. The latest "lean" initiatives, Supply Chain Data Interchange, Set up Reduction, etc., if successful, make for higher efficiencies, higher quality, lower defects, more profits, and more available capacity for growth.

> **Sometimes we trip over excellence:**
> Riverside Precision Sheet Metal is only 10,000 square feet, yet they rival larger shops in revenue. Starting out in the garage behind the owner's home, the shop has been repeatedly expanding to support the growth over the years. "We have three days of Work In Progress, that's it! There is very little room to move in the shop," states the owner. "I like it that way—every job has to move, otherwise it blocks the aisles. It also allows me to see and touch every job as I walk through. "So you practice Just In Time manufacturing?" "What's that?" replied the owner.

Each department may have its own goals and objectives for process execution, but cycle time reduction is typically one of them. Systems used in manufacturing process include not only the ERP system, but PLM solutions for configuration management, and shop floor control systems for material movement and defect tracking.

Planning in smaller manufacturing companies requires less sophisticated scheduling systems. Often, they're just not needed. The microelectronics assembler in NH looks in his miniature, closet-like stock room to see his backlog. Other assemblers use their "gut" and some basic practices that work for them.

> Ken Mar Inc., a 20,000 square foot precision sheet metal shop was being surveyed by Crossfield, an OEM in the imaging industry (this survey occurred in the early '90s, so it is not known how Ken Mar operates today). The shop showed fairly well, had a good compliment of equipment, was clean, had good evidence of quality control, etc. When asked, "How do you plan your capacity?" Ken Mar responded, "Monthly. We take the backlog for each month and schedule the jobs in descending order by dollar value."
>
> The survey team walked away satisfied, except for that comment. By the time the team returned to the office, the conclusion was quite different. "Hey, that's pretty smart!"

This shop sees the same work over and over. Any new business is certainly closely managed through the process for the first build, but on steady state production, the reality is that the highest revenue job has the most volume (machine time), process steps, complexity and outside needs (=lead time) of paint, plating, etc. Then, as the month ticked on, the front end equipment became available for short runs, prototypes, etc.

While this is by no means a foolproof methodology, the rational is fairly sound. There will be the "gotchas" along the way, but much larger shops in various industries run on these types of "gut feel" approaches. Capacity planning can be as simple as above or as complicated as it gets. Larger CMs can develop complex capacity plans, many of which are created in an Excel spreadsheet; others are part of the ERP system.

In larger companies, there are scheduling departments. These are the folks with the antacids jar right out on the desk. They are constantly being challenged with scheduling requests and orders. Some EMS companies have the program manager do the scheduling or work closely with a planner. This creates competition for production line time down on the factory floor. However structured, the planner is the bombardier in the factory, dropping kits to the floor in an effort to keep the pig fed, as it's called. On a perfect day the planner will have a queue in front of the machines with no material shortages and a dead telephone and no e-mail. On any given day, there will be: shortages expedited for kits that are dropped in anticipation of the final components' deliveries, kits that cannot run due to material *surprises* that occur in setting up the job, reschedule requests—both hard reschedules and *what if* scenarios—non conforming materials and quality issues throughout the production process, and typically, a meeting for each subject. The planner's mission is to hit the schedules and, at all costs, keep product moving—the pig is hungry. This is asset utilization.

Real Life:

> *A top 50 EMS provider became so used to materials inaccuracies, that in addition to the material shortage lists and expedite lists, they created a new category, called "Unknown Shortages"! These were the shortages to the kits that mysteriously appeared when the job was about to run, even though the MRP system and the stock room declared it clean and ready to run. The material inaccuracies were so rampant and the efforts to remedy the problem so ineffective, that the EMS company just accepted this as a practice and, just before a kit was run, would generate the list and treat it as an emergency fire drill—daily!*

With the manufacturing line(s) in place, the planning and materials departments now hold the keys to the engine. And, when fired up and with the right people running it, a factory can really rumble. When these factories are cranking it out, the passion comes to the surface. It is those of us who get excited who are the true "Ops" people.

Materials Management / Inventory Control / Supply Chain Execution

> *As it was once humorously put to the customer by the CEO of a $300 million EMS: "My materials manager is in a no-win situation: either the lines will be down, or we will have too much on hand. And, on the one day when everything is just right, I'll tell him he paid too much!"*

Proper inventory management not only helps the CM, but also limits the risks passed on to the customer from schedule shifts and design changes. EMS customers should be keen on this capability—not only for the obvious reasons, but because the outsourcing team is typically headed by the materials department of the OEM, and they can dig right into the detail!

The tool to execute this task is the **MRP (Materials Requirement Planning)** system. This may be part of an ERP (Enterprise Resource Planning system), but the functionality is the same.

The assemblies' bills of materials and the sales orders with the quantities and deliveries are loaded into the MRP system. The MRP then "rolls," and the requirements "net out." The resulting "action report" takes into account all required build schedules, on-hand inventory, on-order inventory and the lead time of the components that are required to satisfy the schedule. The action report will include actions to buy, material schedule pull-ins and push-outs, and cancellations for all items that do not fall in line to support the build schedule.

With some systems or businesses that support a high mix or complex assemblies, the roll of the MRP may be scheduled, or paced, so as not to drive the materials staff crazy. One of the largest challenges for the EMS provider is to maintain accuracy in the MRP with respect to physical on-hand balances (a separate study may be warranted here), as machine scrap and handling issues compound themselves over multiple builds of the same items. The aforementioned case of the unknown shortages list exemplifies this.

One of the big frustrations EMS providers' customers experience is the **internal cycle time to order materials**. In complex PCB assemblies, there are many items to procure and the customer wants to be advised of any potential issues that may impact delivery of the final product. This is a typical milestone requested of the EMS company: a declaration of all materials on order and a listing of any materials with delivery dates that do not support the build schedule. Multiple factors can contribute to a lengthy cycle time.

First, the EMS company may schedule MRP rolls once or twice a week to avoid constant and sometimes repetitive materials scheduling. In recent years, MRP systems have become more sophisticated, and typically net out "on the fly," avoiding the lag time and spike in activity created by a weekly, large MRP dump (actual term). While the newer systems are more sophisticated, many CMs, including EMS providers, are not about to spend the money on a new EPR/MRP when their legacy system is performing adequately. "How often do you 'action' or 'roll' MRP?" is a question frequently asked by a survey team visiting a potential contract manufacturing partner.

Second, the customer data must be entered into the ERP system. The speed at which this is accomplished has several things impacting it:

a) The format in which the customer provides the data (covered later in this study) may be difficult to handle or understand, as well as its degree of completeness.

b) The ERP system may have limitations on importing data, resulting in a worst case scenario of each component, its specification, approved manufacturers (Approved Vendor List, Approved Manufacturers List), and the product structure being keystroked into the MRP manually.

c) The internal process the EMS company follows may have a sequential pathway of review, formatting, and sign off.

d) The people involved in the process also affect speed. There may be a fragmented structure, where purchasing is set up by "commodity" and multiple people have to react to get all components ordered. Also, the workloads of individuals fluctuate in the process. Remember, this is a lean work force.

Once the data is configured and entered and the system "rolls," the buyers can now "action" the MRP and place orders, scheduling materials for the build. Here, problems arise. Components may have availability issues, specs may be incomplete, or pricing may have changed enough to create a *red flag* issue. When the customer is notified of these issues, weeks may have passed from the placement of the order, hence, the frustration.

Real life:
Cooper Perkins of Burlington, MA, is a product design and engineering firm. They often participate in a three-way relationship with their OEM customers and the OEM's chosen contract manufacturer. On one project, all three participants were located less than 90 minutes from each other. The CM, in southeastern Massachusetts, had full process management systems, ISO and FAA certifications, and a full staff (engineering, materials, quality, program management, etc.) to support production and new product introduction. Typical of their projects, Cooper Perkins was to see this one through to production, validating the "design for manufacturability" at the source of manufacturing.

The prototype build was for a few units of several small printed circuit board assemblies. The deliverable to the CM was a documentation package that contained not only all of the necessary specifications, but all of the sources who had the components in stock, the price, and the sales contacts' names and phone numbers. They outlined the plan to the CM, which was for them to order the bare boards with a two-week turnaround (this is an expedited delivery at a premium charge), then secure the rest of the materials, and create the manufacturing process documentation during the two weeks, then build in week 3.

(The above scenario is not uncommon in the industry. In fact, any EMS provider that touts a core competence of new product introduction (most, if not all, do), would have this mapped out in a process flow and perhaps a special team, or at a minimum, special meetings to review new projects coming into production.)

After one week, no parts were on order. The purchasing department responded that they had yet to see any requirements in the MRP system and they would have to wait until the next "roll" (over the next weekend) to see if the requirements were loaded. The engineer from Cooper Perkins pulled the job, drove to a small CM (Wire Techniques, mentioned elsewhere in this study), and handed the job to them. The purchasing agent called all of the sources on the list, placing the orders in one day, and loaded the MRP the next day with all of the component orders.

The need for speed and flexibility can bump into the traditional mindset of how things are done at a CM. And, if there is a bureaucracy to be navigated, it can be downright impossible to achieve what one might perceive as reasonable responsiveness. The larger CM grew out of the defense contracting arena, where it is important to note the year, not just the day and month on everything.

Proper **materials management** is absolutely "business critical" to the EMS company. For today, ignore *Accounting 101* and consider inventory a "liability," not an "asset." Things now start to become very clear. Inventory, unless moving quickly through the factory, is evil. Certain levels of inventory must be on hand to conduct business, such as minimum buys and components packaged in volume—necessary evil. Pure excess inventory—material on hand that will not be consumed by the backlog in the MRP—is the absolute devil.

Limiting excess inventory is critical to turning the total bucket, and turning the buckets makes the EMS company tick. Inventory is cash, and the less tied up it is, the better.

For automated assembly, the components are packed in reels. These volumes can be in the thousands and, while most are very inexpensive (less than a penny,) some are not. Other items are packaged in tubes and trays and can be in the hundreds. These can be "B" class and even "A" items (expensive.) If a products annual usage is low, years of inventory may be bought just for the initial pilot run.

A watchful eye on excess can result in paying a little more, but eliminating risk. If properly done, these decisions will happen in the quote stage- so the standards are set properly and margin is not eroded (more on this later). After a downturn in the economy, this becomes a front burner issue, as the customers are ordering in smaller lots and the CM's are limiting risk. Cut reels, or mini reels, for example, are becoming more popular. The unit prices are slightly higher, but the risk is eliminated.

Fabrication shops (job shops) use common material for multiple customers, mostly eliminating unusable excess material at the end of program. Their liabilities are typically in finished goods from building ahead or from an overrun. Also, maintaining adequate levels of raw stock at a machine shop or sheet metal fabricator is typically not financially crippling. EMS providers, on the other hand—**remember the 70/30 rule**—buy tremendous amounts of standard and custom material (from the job shops) to support orders from their customers. Often, there are minimums that must be purchased, such as reels of up to 3000 components (to feed auto placement machines). A significant excess inventory position is a powder keg waiting to go off.

Also, not only does material make up 70% of the sell price, but any unfavorable PPV *(Purchase Price Variance, defined as the difference between the targeted or standard cost and the actual cost paid for components)* will quickly erode the already thin profits established in the cost model. To hedge this, the materials staff is focused on pricing variances.

> In many EMS providers, the materials staff is often measured on and compensated for:
> On-time delivery (from suppliers)
> Incoming inspection grades
> PPV
> Cost reductions/savings

The above **goals** are from a traditional mindset. If the suppliers are on time, then in theory, the factory runs smoothly and the customers are happy, and so on. These metrics and objectives set the **behavior** of the staff, as there may be a bonus riding on achieving certain targets. While these are key elements to the financial performance of the company, when listed as personal objectives, the enterprise's best interests can move to the bottom of the list.

Supplier delivery dates may be meticulously adjusted to keep suppliers on time with their commits, but may not reflect the on-time production starts. Quality performance reduces costs and workflow interruptions, but again, the numbers can be "managed" to keep the statistics showing what management wants to see.

> In the example above, Cooper Perkins pulled the job after a week of no evidence of progress to get parts on order, even after supplying clean documentation with all of the sourcing information. Even if this information was loaded into the MRP and "actioned," the CM's purchasing manager had a bonus incentive on PPV objectives. On other programs at this CM, programs would be won and launched, but the bidding process would start over, driving the distributors crazy, as they had just bid the parts to create the winning proposal. The purchasing manager was not about to let customer delivery dates, the new product introduction process, or any streamlined process get in the way of a chance at making a bonus!

PPV and cost savings are related, but not necessarily the same. If the latest market/actual price is entered and the standard cost is updated, the favorable PPV is eliminated. But, since the total COGS number went down, the profit margin increased. This may be tracked elsewhere as a cost savings, as there is no longer evidence of the efforts. Also, cost reductions may be passed on in part or in whole to the customer, not affecting the bottom line, but adding to responsiveness, customer satisfaction, and competitiveness in the industry.

As the industry has evolved, expertise has as well. Vendors are now called "supply chain partners," or a dozen other trendy acronyms. And, like the CM, the vendor is looking for hard orders. Managing this non-committed forecast from the OEM on downstream through the supply chain has its intricacies.

In larger EMS providers, strategic initiatives come into play. Commodity level expertise for sourcing decisions, EDI links, in-house stores and Volume Purchase Agreements (VPA) can be employed, if the EMS company has a sufficient volume of business.

Typically, **supply chain management programs** will not commit to a purchase of the total projected volume (called estimated annual usage, or EAU) but just award orders, as needed, if they materialize, to a selected supplier at a price. The rest of it all deals with how much inventory is available, where it is located, and how it is released when the commitments are made. If there is an abnormally long lead time for a component, then a **bond** may be put in place for strategic components—with the OEM's approval and ultimate responsibility for the liability to have the component available to support the build plan.

In house stores, or in house stocking programs put the distributor inside the CM. If large enough, it will be staffed by the distributor's employees. The benefit to the distributor is that they have a lock on the business. The benefit to the CM is that they are only invoiced for parts as they are consumed. This takes away planning errors or the inability to react quickly to schedule shifts and the purchasing of the entire reel of parts when just a few are needed. There is also a tremendous administrative gain: no processing of material through receiving and inspection, and accounting is streamlined as well.

A **Volume Purchase Agreement, or VPA** is one where a supplier agrees to certain terms for a certain dollar volume of business. This usually appears in the form of a rebate to the CM after a certain dollar volume is achieved. This is also known as *Plateau Agreement*.

Negotiating the supply chain has its intricacies, too. For the EMS industry, the manufacturers of the components solicit the OEM—to be "designed into" the products. The mentality used to be, as quoted from a marketing executive at the world's largest distributor at the time, "We work at the OEM level to get the business, then it's just a question of where the orders come from (at the CM level)." This remains true for the expensive "A" items of microprocessors and "chip sets" of certain manufacturers. Although several distributors may carry the same manufacturer's products, the sales efforts at the OEM result in one distributor establishing a **"registration"** for a given component when purchased by/on behalf of a given OEM. This typically results in a special price that the other distributors cannot touch, sometimes involving a rebate from the manufacturer to the distributor.

For the balance of the components, the distributors must now compete for the EMS provider's business. As mentioned earlier in this study, distributors, as well as the job shop, must now follow their initial efforts with the OEMs into the EMS provider and, at times, win it all over again. After all, the EMS provider has preferred relationships, stocking programs, possible incentives for volume business, as well as approved custom fabricators—PCBs, metal, and cable assemblies—pushing the OEM to use their sources.

Some OEMs are using E-bids, or **reverse auctions,** to award their business. This is a live, web-based event, where the low bid at the bell takes all. This is covered in more detail in the review of the OEM. For the EMS provider, there is a strong resistance from the component suppliers to participate is such an event, thus, it is presently not a common practice.

The quest for strategic materials management and cost reduction programs can be next to impossible, with the daily shortages and required reactions to schedule shifts consuming available resources. And, in the middle of it all, the end of the quarter rolls in and all eyes are 24/7 on the revenue line and the excess position, abandoning—at least for the moment—any best practice or streamlined process implementation.

The competencies that a CM must possess can be generalized as the ability to consistently and efficiently perform their skills and execute related business processes. Balance and execution not only equal responsiveness (read: customer satisfaction), but also create profits. The typical sales pitch provides the position statement, "Why bother when we can do it better, faster, and cheaper, because that's what we do for living."

7. Risk Management

EMS providers are getting better at analyzing and communicating with their supply chains. "What if" scenarios now exist and the supply chain participates more as a partner to them (rather than just to the OEM), so all is not lost. But if you buy parts, make sure you have a purchase order or a contract that does a nice job in the CYA department.

In the event of an ECO (Engineering Change Order), the customer will (should) be liable for those on-hand components' inventory of items deleted from the design, plus (Work In Progress) rework charges at the point of both parties agreeing to the changes. Typically, the customer will issue a purchase order for the materials impact and any rework. If different, the product costing is adjusted at this point.

In the event of a purchase order cancellation, that fast moving inventory stops dead and instantly becomes liability/risk. Some raw components may be returned for credit, while anything custom or with value added to it cannot. Clear rules must be in place with respect to the downside.

To limit risk and manage liability in the relationship, the program manager/account manager is typically the responsible party or watchdog, often joined at the hip with the materials department. Quick response to change, documenting issues and liability, and periodic reviews to monitor excess inventory positions and additional costs, will keep the relationship on an even keel. This is often overlooked, however, especially when business is good, as the customer keeps cranking out orders and the factory keeps humming along, often pushing issues aside. The good contract administrator will mind the rules, issues, and keep the liabilities on the front burner. The customer will appreciate the pushing back—in the long run.

This seems so basic that only those in the lowest tier must not be practicing this, right?

In the late '90s, a large telecom represented $50+/- million in annual revenue—over many years—to a $200+ million EMS company. Resultant from mergers and acquisitions, the OEM's new corporate parent advised that the business would be moved to another EMS company. Quite a mess ensued. There was litigation and a trial for millions of dollars (costing millions of dollars) over residual inventory. Both sides were adamant about the other's liability.

Of note: there was over $600K in component inventory pertaining to ECOs, which had never been recouped from the customer. These parts were typically programmed ICs and became scrap as the designs changed and new programmed chips were spec'd in. Amidst all the good times, engineering changes were rampant, and ECOs were quickly executed, albeit, never completely reconciled by the CM. While the OEM was contractually liable for the parts, how can you go back, after several years, and ask for such a large check? Proper account management would have brought timely closure to the financial aspects of the changes, reducing the inevitable claim by a decent chunk.

The customer, too, can pose a risk to the contract manufacturer. Should they go bankrupt, the CM is left holding the bag on receivables, WIP, and raw materials.

So, while the CM may be hungry for business, they must be cautious about who they do business with, because it could lead to disaster. In the '90s, SCI had many facilities, but a centralized "asset manager" approved all customers. For start up companies and those the manager determined were a risk, a "standby letter of credit" (which basically escrowed funds for the risk amount) was demanded. The amount was described as the "30/60/90" rule, where the program's annual dollar value would consider three months to be escrowed. At any point in time, there would be 30 days of outstanding receivables, 30 days of WIP, and 30 days of raw materials on hand to support the schedule. This would be the minimum amount at risk.

More and more, EMS providers are demanding cash in advance. This used to be a policy seen only for offshore sourcing efforts. But after the bloodbath of 2001, EMS providers may demand up to 50% down (to cover the majority of material purchases, then COD for the balance) until a comfort level has been established with the new customer.

8. Quality Systems

Quality is often the most investigated attribute when evaluating a CM for any service. **Quality plans** and manuals document processes and controls throughout the enterprise. Smaller manufacturers may possess specialized skills and be able to manufacture to a very high degree of difficulty, yet they do not document quality control processes—or maybe even have them. This makes the manufacturer a niche player, because they cannot pass a typical audit from a typical manufacturer, even though they may be the best in the business at their skills. But, unless special waivers or conditions are put in place, the door is closed to many potential customers, as the customer's quality manual has an approval process for suppliers that must be adhered to.

Thus, we see smaller contract manufacturers and the job shops maintaining ISO certifications, as well as FAA, UL, FDA, and other certifications, which come with cost to the enterprise. Lack of these can be a red flag for an OEM, regardless of ability, so to maintain an approved status or qualify for new business the CMs put these governance programs in place.

Back in the Stone Age, there was Mil-I 45208/B, the inspection standard for doing business with the DOD. In the '90s ISO 9000/9001 standards became the trend. ISO 9001 was more for OEMs, as it added standards and controls on product design as well as the manufacturing of products covered under ISO 9000. The CMs typically chose to be 9000 approved. To become approved, a company had to define many processes and their control. To document enforcement, there had to be ongoing monitoring/auditing of the system documenting corrective action on nonconformance issues. The system as a whole was then subject to an outside agency's (read: at cost) inspection and approval. This approval was not only costly to establish, but the outside agency must be brought back into the CM for follow up on surveillance audits.

More and more, the DOD has given way to the ISO standards as the minimum requirement. Old and new standards, such as AS14000, have spawned a new industry of consultants, providing a gap analysis on what it would take to get a company approved, all the way through to establishing the infrastructure and conducting pre-assessment audits.

Within these heavily documented procedures and controls is the meat of the quality system. The ISO system is one that documents that you have and follow a given procedure, not that it is necessarily the right procedure. It is under this layer that the true ability of a manufacturer can be determined. A material control system may be defined and successfully audited, but the questions are: Does it provide for proper handling of defective material? Have a closed loop corrective action procedure? Provide quick remedy for materials issues, etc.?

Other policies and procedures cover calibration and preventative maintenance of equipment, certification and training of the labor force, incoming inspection and acceptance procedures, and maintaining and analyzing of quality data from the factory floor. This yield and defect tracking methods scale in sophistication with the size of the contract manufacture. A small cable assembly shop or sheet metal fabricator may write down quality information on the shop floor traveler (work instructions), which is then read the next time the job is released, or sent to the front office for resolution. In larger shops, we can find Statistical Process Control (SPC) utilized to monitor problems or critical processes that can have varying results. SPC is a mapping of data points with outer limits and trend analysis to maintain an "in control" status. Drift too far in the wrong direction or exceed a boundary and the process is declared out of control and must be immediately stopped for root cause analysis and corrective action. In an EMS company, the front end of PBC assembly requires the solder pasting of the raw circuit boards. Here the volume of the paste is critical to back end test yields. SPC at the front end of the manufacturing line is better than watching things go wrong in test. Of course, test yields are monitored as well, since there are more process steps that can introduce defects as products move through the factory.

Both above practices can work very well. In fact, both can be part of an ISO approved system, providing they are well documented and adhered to (with evidence).

And, like all of the other attributes of the manufacturing company, at the heart of this one are the people. Basic human behavior can result in perfection or disaster using the same set of systems and processes.

The stories are numerous:

EMS Provider
In the '90s a plant manager for a SCI read something about world-class manufacturing and declared that they would build quality into the products at each work center and, in one breath, eliminated final inspection. Not only was there a massive product return from the customer base, but it was found that an assembler was color blind, not being able to confirm the value of the through hole components (color-coded) he was assembling and now inspecting.

Machine Shop
In the process of machining castings, a threaded insert called a "helicoil" is inserted into the machined screw holes. The "tang" inside the coil aids in insertion and is snipped off after installation. Triple A Manufacturing supported United Technologies in the '80s and '90s. They did not know about the snipping requirement and, when on a visit to UTC, was cornered by the production manager: "Why do we have to snip the helicoil tangs?"
The product was accepted "as is" (no notification to the supplier) and the snipping was done by the shop floor—for over two years!

Plastics
A plastics molder makes very small plastic parts for the packaging of consumer spray products, in very high volume. When a follow-on order came in for a given item, the master scheduler noted that

there were 80,000 in stock. Thus, the requirement of 300,000 needed only a 220,000 kit drop. "No," he was told. "We need to drop 300,000 because the 80,000 are defective." "Then scrap them," the master scheduler advised the planning team. "No, we can't; our quality rating will go down." The individual goals the company placed on the quality manager caused actions that corrupted the ERP system, hid financial liability, and allowed for more defective product to be built by not addressing the root cause of the defective production lot.

EMS Provider
SCI was awarded a job to assemble microprocessors consigned by IBM to small circuit boards. The testing of the boards was very simple: place the board on a large, grid-like socket and turn on. If it lights up green, it passes; red, it fails. The second shift operator was new and did not line up the pins to the right rows, slightly skewing the mounting. Over 190 blown microprocessors later, her shift ended. "They just kept failing," she said.

Procedures and process controls can be reviewed in the company's quality plan, which documents how the company executes and controls their manufacturing, as well as business processes.

How <u>well</u> the CM executes on these is the million dollar question. With multiple customers, multiple products, and multiple daily needs, a balancing act is required to satisfy all needs, for all customers, every day. The higher the mix, the tougher this is to sustain.

9. Competitiveness

Wherever you land on the "service vs. volume" scale, you must still remain cost competitive within your market segment. Controlling or reducing costs is one of the main reasons companies look to outsource. Many OEMs benchmark pricing during product development and, from time to time, during the production relationship, by quoting your competitors.

What gets built into the cost model is the "degree of difficulty." For shops that specialize in quick turn prototyping and high mix production, the responsiveness is set very high, while the factory efficiency is set very low, and the pricing model appropriately addresses this with much higher labor rates (or lower efficiency rates). Large volume programs are not as "light on their feet," with the factory running more efficiently, thus, the pricing model will be much more aggressive—with lower margin, but higher revenues per product. Here, the customer will have to stick to the rules and have firm schedules, with longer planning horizons.

Some CMs specialize in more technical processes, tests and engineering. This ability comes with cost. But, if an OEM recognizes their ability to get to market will be greatly enhanced, they may pay the price.

Plexus of Wisconsin is an option. Plexus evolved with an engineering services core competence. This generates larger profits, plus gives them an edge in getting their customers to market. Many telecom companies have enjoyed great success with Plexus. Not only could the CM participate in the design of the PCBs, but the factory was set up to be very responsive to new product introduction needs. Scheduling and program management were staffed more heavily to support the customers. The results were/are impressive.

Around 2000, technology companies in the Northeastern corridor (Boston area) had wide-open options. The big telecoms could place their business at almost any CM, as the big dogs were all now local: Jabil, SCI-Sanmina, Solectron, Benchmark, Celestica, and ACT all had full up, large production facilities within 30–40 miles of downtown Boston. And these were just the billion dollar CMs in the area.

So, why would any telecom, start up or not, choose to go all the way to Neenah, Wisconsin? When a manager at one of these telecoms (who had previously been a program manager at a large EMS provider) was asked why, he responded: "How about a WIP (Work In Progress) report, delivery schedule and action item list updated and e-mailed to me by 9 every morning without asking?" This was unheard of. Plus, they excelled at PCB design/layout, which could be offloaded to them. The model was successful and became more popular as various OEM's staff moved about in the local market. Plexus has since acquired a CM in the Boston area and created an NPI center—and now closed it, due to market conditions!

How do they do this? **price, service, quality** . . . pick two!

You get what you pay for, and Plexus is not cheap. It's a different model and there are different services to enhance the model, including product development and high end military work. All of these have cost models that can provide the added infrastructure to proved exceptional support.

Plexus is an "A" player, and venture-backed start ups and larger OEMs will often fund this model, because it presents a significant reduction in risk in *time to market*.

10. Financial Performance

Quote Equals Standard

Repeat 1000 times. What you told the customer it would take to make their product becomes the standard. Maybe the customer only sees the final number, but it contains all of the content to build the product and make a profit, and thus becomes the standard by which the factory will be measured. And while there may be some companies that employ another "internal" set of numbers that add overhead or hide profit, we won't complicate life at this point.

The logic of standard costs at SCI in the '90s-
Say this loudly while banging your fist on the desk: *"If your quote shows the part at a buck, then the standard is a buck! If Purchasing buys it for 50 cents, it's called PPV! If Purchasing buys it for two bucks, you're fired!"*

Often, in the EMS industry, the cost model is shared with the customer, providing a complete breakdown of how the sell price is calculated, including the cost of all materials, via "costed BOMs." Why would one share such a confidential, business critical document with a customer? Some don't. But, in many large, multi-million dollar relationships, it's the model that gets negotiated up front, then business is much easier to conduct, streamlining new product launches and standardizing the agenda for cost reviews. Once negotiated, the quoted and actual costs can be jointly reviewed for pricing issues and cost reduction opportunities. This also eliminates the "hiding" of costs or inflating of prices by the CM. Also, most OEMs know what their products' material content is and have a decent understanding of the labor content. Their product team quotes the components during development, and has its own internal numbers to hit. If the CM quote comes in too high, the cost issues get attacked by the team, not the CM's profit (on the first round, anyway).

All of this upfront model building, negotiating, and data sharing will make the front end of doing business run smoothly; it will, however result in a PPV of 0%, as costs will match the standards. During the execution phase, the goals placed on the materials department can drive them to revisit and renegotiate cost at the expense of the product launch, as mentioned prior. This can have a tremendously negative impact with the customer.

The quote to the customer will set the standards that are then monitored for variances against the actual times and expenditures recorded in the execution of the purchase orders. Thus, a good quote model will mimic the company's P&L report.

Creating the quotation is the first step in contract manufacturing, yet it exercises every core competence the enterprise possesses.

As with process standardization and control covered in the manufacturing core competence section, we follow the same logic, as the customer documentation arrives in variable formats. It may consist of electronic data with CAD drawings, PLM solution's export of a bill of material into an Excel or other format, PDF files with specifications, or a combination of the above and more. (This is covered in more detail in "Design and Documentation for Manufacturing.") The quoting specialist (who may wear multiple hats in the organization, or report to various departments, depending on which CM you are studying) must analyze the documentation for completeness and then route it through the disciplines and systems within the enterprise to gather accurate manufacturing information. Materials must query the supply chain for raw materials and component pricing, noting availability and minimum order commitments. Engineering skills must be employed to confirm the ability to perform the required manufacturing steps and establish times for each operation as well as any NRE costs (Non-Recurring Engineering, AKA tooling). Executive management must assign or approve the cost rates, overheads, and profit assigned to the proposal. And, finally, Marketing/Sales, or Business Development must deliver a response to the customer.

The quote delivered back to the customer may be in many formats, from a verbal communication or simple e-mail, on up to a many paged, in-depth manufacturing proposal. The job shops tend to keep it simple, responding with a total price per unit and any applicable NRE or set up. This can be done on one page, with some notes regarding lead time and payment terms. The EMS proposals tend to be in much more depth, and customers are more interested in the content that totals to the final price, as these awards can be very large. The sales/marketing role is to ensure the proposal is professional, comprehensive—providing the information the customer is requesting—profitable, and notes liability and any exceptions. This will be the template for standard setting if the job is won.

Conversion costs are calculated by taking the sell price from the CM and subtracting the material cost (to the CM). That number is the cost to convert the material into the ship level product. Many OEMs look at this to sanity check the models, while others look for a target percentage.

> Bay Networks was outsourcing tens of millions of dollars to ACT Manufacturing in the late '90s. They were not the only CM supporting Bay. The call then came for a 9% conversion cost on the next round of bidding. The rational was that there was such a high material content to the assemblies—some in excess of $5000—that labor was insignificant, and an easy 7% could be made on millions of dollars of revenue. It is not known how successful this effort was, but it was certainly a bold one.

Whatever the model, it is these numbers that must be set as the standards—these numbers which will be measured against the factory's actuals.

Set the Standard

The "roll up" of the standard costs of an assembly is the total cost to the enterprise to make it. When a new job is won, these standards are entered into the ERP system and, for each unit shipped, the revenue is then declared, as well as the cost content from the standards. As mentioned above, as a practice, the "quoted cost" should equal the "standard cost." If the cost of a connector is $1.00 and you apply a 25% profit to it to sell to the customer, the standard cost should be $1.00. The cost model should be consistent. The "sell price", minus the cost roll up, equals **gross profit.** Again, in the EMS world, the customer often quotes the components themselves to benchmark the design, and compares the cost detail in the responses from multiple bidders.

Labor "paid" (actual) and "sold" (standard) is a result of hours, multiplied by an hourly rate. Or, a process step (which has a standard) times a rate, such as a cut or punch on metal, a placement of a component on a PCB, or a crimp of a wire on a connector. Individual process steps can be analyzed for efficiency by looking at the variances. But to do this, a very sophisticated system must be in place. WIP tracking and shop floor control systems will have reporting mechanisms that can be utilized for this, but the integrity of the data will lie in the employees reporting accurate times spent on jobs.

Other standards include **overhead**, which is typically a percentage of labor, and **other** costs.

Changing a standard may result from a negotiation with the supply chain, a change in market price of given components, or a change in the labor due to an ECO or review of actual data. When changing these standards, caution must be taken with regard to the impact to inventory and work in process. The materials must be reviewed for "on-hand" quantity, as well as the committed orders pricing. Updating the standards causes a "reval" (revaluation) of the financial (asset) value of the inventory.

If done right, everything will wash in the bottom line:

Example: If there were 500 parts in stock at $1 and the standard was changed to $2, the value of the inventory would rise to $1000. If the parts were bought for $1, then there is a temporary gain in the "reval." Once the materials are consumed in manufacturing and "sold" to the customer, the gain is offset, as the cost of goods sold is now higher—at $2—and the remaining profit is now $1 lower. That is, unless the price to the customer was adjusted for the price increase. This pricing "cut in" should be targeted based on the inventory's consumption; if it is done too early, more profits, if done late, less.

Monitor the Variance

If you end up buying that $1 part for $0.50, the "favorable" PPV (Purchase Price Variance) goes right to the bottom line. The materials staff will have a watchful eye on this, and, for the most part, those items with large favorable variances (for whatever reason) may go unaddressed, as they help the department's cause and bolster their performance stats. Negative variances are "front burner" issues and can hold up schedules until they get resolved. Not a bad practice considering a variance on an "A" item could jeopardize the profitability of the project, but the favorable variances could be hiding another issue.

Real life:
A small CM in Springfield, MA, had a purchasing staff of 4–5 people. The system reports stated that materials purchases were yielding a favorable overall variance of 7–8%. Digging into the data revealed that there was one part (flex circuit) with a standard cost of $350.00 and was bought for $225, every time. That's $125 favorable PPV, and the component's usage was in the hundreds. The labor was $50.00 for each assembly, which was very profitable. A look at the PO from the end customer had a unit price of $400 each.

The above data shows the job to be a loser—the costs being larger than the sell price (there were a couple of other parts totaling another ten or so dollars). But the job yielded a ton of favorable PPV.

The reality was that the flex circuit was second sourced for a cost reduction and some of the savings were passed on to the customer. The standard cost of the connector was never changed, resulting in

> a COGS of over $400 with a sell price of $400. All of the profit on the job was in the PPV "bucket."
>
> If the standards were corrected, we would see something like:
> $225 flex circuit
> $12 other material
> $50 labor
>
> $287 Cost, with $113 profit. A very profitable job!
>
> The numbers were too large for the purchasing manager not to notice the standard cost had not been changed. But, if you were being measured every day and this was running in the background juicing your performance statistics, would you bring it up?

While the above scenario does not impact the bottom line of the company, it clouds data, hiding other issues affecting profitability—mainly purchasing performance! Materials variance monitoring should be an ongoing effort by the enterprise—not only to keep things on the favorable side of the variance, but to keep pricing accurate in a competitive market.

> In the '90s SCI was reported to target a 2% favorable PPV. This added to the bottom line but did not drive the company down a different road in the goals and objectives department. The objective was to keep the standards as close to reality and thus bid business as competitively as possible.

On the **labor** side, if you bid one hour to build the job and set the standard accordingly, and it then takes two hours, you are 50% efficient to the standard. This is an unfavorable variance, providing the labor rates are equal. Of course, if you doubled the rate in the bid, all is the same.

Big variance swings can come as surprises. The **overhead** variance is volatile because it is tied to a projected average number of hours of labor to be sold (billed in shipments) each month, and that number is then divided into the average projected monthly dollars it takes to run the facility.

The projected hours are typically a (high) percentage of the available hours of labor that can be sold/billed by the factory (total capacity), where efficiencies, utilization, and the backlog numbers are factored in to make the prediction. If revenues fall short of the projection, the overhead expense is now spread out over fewer hours (sold) and an unfavorable variance occurs. The labor variance also takes a hit, but Labor is a variable and can be better managed—perhaps people were sent home, overtime was eliminated, or vacations were forced due to a foreseen slow down. Both take the maximum hit when there is no slow down, the shop is busy, and something holds up a large shipment—where the investment had been made—but sees no relief or absorption of costs on the revenue side. In these cases a **reserve** can be taken in the form of a temporary credit against the next financial period, which will be very profitable with a lot of initial revenue achieved without expenses.

Add any unexpected overhead cost to the above scenario and your financial period becomes a smoking crater. This is where reserves must be used to their fullest.

Variance monitoring enables the enterprise to hone processes, identify issues, and drive cost reduction in the factory, front office, and throughout the supply chain.

> *PictureTel Corporation built a PC-style box at SCI:*
> *The order kicked off smoothly, with a minimal amount of ECO activity; there was a $2500 ECO fund (described later) that had not been consumed, and PictureTel didn't care, because the launch was successful. At the end of each month, however, the account was a loser. Every month, in fact, a $1000–$3000 loss was posted. There were only two products being built for PictureTel, so the investigation began. The standards were good. Not only was the $2500 slush fund intact, but also extra costs to program ICs at a subcontractor were entered and these "other costs" were tracked in the standards roll*

up. The second product was right on the money; it was just introduced and the numbers were good.

The loss was from an unfavorable labor variance. But the labor numbers tracked back to the original labor quote. The Ops manager confirmed the throughput of the 100 motherboards was well under standard and the box level assembly and test should be within standard as well.

The investigation drilled down to the time cards. There was a two-week lull where no PictureTel products were built. Yet, 80 hours were charged to the customer work order. It seems Helen (not her real name) was not properly trained on how to fill out her time card. She did not know any better and kept filling in the first work order number they gave—every day of every week, regardless of what she was working on. Helen worked in the "through hole" assembly area and none of PictureTel's products had any "through hole" labor content!

The above example shows that the numbers are only as good as those entering the data. But when the detail is available, reconciling the P&L can be a fruitful experience. All other costs should be calculated and documented during the quote phase so that an accurate profit margin can be detailed during P&L reporting. This will flush out the inefficiencies in execution and create an environment for successful problem solving.

Overhead variance, while a bit of a catch all, sums up a lot of expense that can be minimized, or otherwise contained. And it also shows how not shipping enough revenue can quickly hurt a large operation; the income dollars are needed to absorb (pay for) the overhead.

Sometimes, these variances come out of the woodwork unexpectedly. And, when they are large, there is often an inquisition as to how they occurred, as they are now "actuals" and the hit has been taken. At the end of the day, sometimes the price needs to go up to make things work. The customer does not want to hear that, and the account manager does not want to deliver the bad news. Sometimes it has to happen to fix an acute problem: a missed item in the cost roll up, an unplanned-for process step, or a supplier raising the price on raw materials. Sometimes there is a more general problem to fix:

> While PictureTel ran two small products, SCI's "600-pound gorilla" was Racal Interlan. Once SCI's largest customer, Racal had slipped to the number two slot in revenue and had a relatively large mix of moderate volume products. Their high volume products were sourced overseas, except for one, which SCI ran half the volume for to ensure availability. All products were negotiated quarterly, and brutally. "C" class items, those parts worth less than 10 cents, were "only" looked at semiannually. Everything else was under scrutiny every three months. The high volume product was repeatedly threatened to be taken completely offshore if their price targets were not met. Racal was also ECO-happy, launching a change a day, on average.
>
> Finally, at a quarterly business review, SCI gave a different presentation. Rather than the overview of business metrics: quality, on-time delivery, etc., the lead program manager presented the P&L for their account. A consistent 10%–13% loss had been posted, every month. Their purchasing manager did not want to hear any of this and was anxious to get started negotiating his "price drivers." It was explained again, politely, that the account was a loser.
>
> No matter what was said or done in these "cost/price driver" meetings, the amount of ECOs, schedule shifts, and unfavorable PPV, created inefficiencies that required an across-the-board 15% price increase just to stabilize the program to the break even point. Racal protested. SCI said work must then stop. So, Racal paid the increase, then, as predicted, moved their business within 6 months and undoubtedly tortured another CM, until Racal eventually vanished from the telecom scene.

Truth be known, SCI waited a long time to tell Racal to piss off. Starting out, Racal was the largest customer, and they called the shots—to the point of a loss. But the factory had been built for $40+ million in revenue and they were far from it, so the prospects of losing them had more of an impact to the P&L than running at a loss, being faced with complete downtime without the Racal orders. Finally, they saw their revenue grow to the point where they no longer needed the overhead absorption and could be profitable on all of the other business without the asset utilization Racal created.

P&L Reporting

Remember, at a CM there is no new gizmo being invented that will send revenue through the roof. It is the CM's performance against the standards (which were created when bidding the job to the customer) that creates the upside. The monitoring of this performance follows a basic P&L format.

There are the costs to operate the facility, plus fees such as insurance and healthcare benefits, as well as the variable costs of energy, factory supplies, etc. These are called "**indirect costs.**" Also included are the wages of those employees not directly involved in the manufacturing of the products (i.e., management, human resources department, engineering, etc.)

The "**direct costs**" have standards associated with them and are the things required to manufacture the products. These get loaded into the ERP/MRP system. The total of the direct costs (standards) for the products manufactured are then reconciled against the actual data at a given time period's close. The variance to the standards adds profit or erodes profit in the time period.

Indirect costs get categorized into an **"overhead"** number, typically added as a percentage of the labor rate, which is added to the bid (and standard costs). Like material and other costs, it is "sold" in each unit. The P&L report is then created with all costs and expenditures, tallying up to the famous "bottom line."

Example:

Your company manufactures a widget that has a material cost of $100, a labor cost of $25, overhead on labor of 100% / $25 (comes from all the fixed and indirect costs), and sell price of $175, for a profit of $25 dollars (14%). If you sold 1000 of them in the time period, them the P&L report will show:

Revenue:	$175,000
Material @STD (sold):	$100,000
Labor @STD (sold):	$25,000
O/H factor (sold):	$25,000
Cost of goods sold:	$150,000 (material + labor + overhead)
Gross margin:	$25,000 (revenue, less COGS)

Now we load into the model what actually happened, starting with the materials:

Starting inventory (at standard cost):$1,000,000
Material purchases:
At standard:	$150,000
Actual:	$160,000
PPV:	($10,000)

Ending inventory (at standard cost): $1,050,000

It cost $160,000 to raise the inventory asset by $150,000 at standard (remember, $100,000 of material shipped/sold, thus the ending inventory number of $1,050,000), so a $10,000 expense/loss must be taken to reconcile the unfavorable purchasing price variance (more was paid for the material than the standard costs it will be on the books—and sold for.)

Labor can also torpedo the bottom line:

Labor sold (std.):	$25,000
Labor paid (actual):	$30,000
Labor variance:	($5,000)

If the labor rate is $25/hr, each unit shipped (1000) contained an hour of labor (standard).

But, as displayed above, the actual payroll dollars spent on shop labor were $5000 more for the time period, thus creating a negative variance. This can be from inefficiencies, downtime, overtime premiums, or issues such as defects or material shortages that may keep product that had labor invested into it from shipping and becoming revenue dollars. If this were the case, and there were another 200 units that were built, but did not ship—let's say the shipping department (indirect cost) ran out of the special boxes required for shipment—the $5000 would be accounted for (paid) but not credited (sold) in the given month. The good news is that the next month, the units will ship with zero labor (paid), causing the variance to swing the other way.

Adjustments called **reserves** can be taken to keep things smooth, as it all eventually shakes out—a month of loss, then a month of above average profits.

Along with labor, the ***overhead variance*** can be severely damage financial performance. Revenue is critical to overhead variance, as the more you ship, the more overhead you "sell" and thus absorb (a relatively fixed number is being diluted as a percentage of revenue, captured in the *labor sold* bucket).

As stated earlier, *overhead* is the fixed and indirect costs of the facility, including insurance, and staff, or indirect employees, where the job's function does not directly apply/add value to the manufacturing process. Human Resources, Accounting, Purchasing, and higher levels of factory supervision are all examples of indirect costs.

Sometimes reserves are taken here, where the costs are spread out over multiple time periods, or a predicted or known future cost is bankrolled in advance. For example, storm damage to the facility results in a $25,000 repair bill. If there was no previous variance, there is now a $25,000 hit to the bottom line. This could be spread out over

5 months by taking a negative $25,000 reserve on the statement, and a $5000 hit each month to bleed it off, lowering profits, but not taking you into the red.

The reverse could happen as well. If an exceptionally high month of revenue *sold* a tremendous amount of labor and overhead, the variance would look great, yielding extra profits. But, say there was a team of temporary workers that came in to help—and that bill was about to be received—in the next financial period.

Assuming no storm, no temps, and no variance, the above P&L now accounts for the materials loss and the labor variance, resulting in a net profit of $10,000, or 6%.

Some models will break out **SG&A** and material overhead from total overhead. SG&A stands for Sales (including commissions), General, and Administration costs. These are "front office" costs and, if broken out, will take a separate chunk out of the gross profit. These costs can be as much as 7% of sell price, or more, depending upon the company. **Material overhead** is the total of costs related to shipping, receiving, inspecting, and storing of raw materials. For an EMS company, these are typically 2–4%. Either of these can be broken out in the P&L, as well as structured in the bid or estimate, and their resulting actuals can be compared and reconciled as a variance.

Other costs show up as *"direct"* and *"indirect"* costs. Other costs that are direct are charges applied to a work order or customer account. An outside service, such as plating or the programming of ICs, show up as an expense for manufacturing products that are not tied to inventory or labor.

Other costs that are indirect are like the storm damage mentioned above or other unplanned nor budgeted (in overhead expense) items. Interest, debt, long term depreciation, and taxes all roll into the P&L and affect the gross margin, but this study is about manufacturing performance, so we will not take the reporting to that level of detail.

In each manufacturing company, financial reporting sees different levels of detail, depending on the need to know and the supporting system's ability to provide it. At SCI in the '90s, the system had some limitations. The program managers were responsible for the P&L for their given customers. Thus, all business was quoted by the PMs, and the resulting standards were set by them as well. The limiter was that each customer was a "work order" number and all products built under that customer were merged into total numbers, limiting the ability to reconcile some of the unfavorable variances.

The program manager also presented the numbers (P&L) to the staff for his or her respective customers. In order to answer to the numbers—sometimes bad numbers—the program manager would set detailed standards, ensuring the cost structure supported the business models and quotes.

> *PictureTel had SCI building a new box level product (basically a PC) at 100 units per month. The sell price was inflated by $25/ea., for the first 100 units. This was built-in as a little slush fund—to be used for the costs associated with ECOs that were pending on the new product launch and to eliminate stopping and quoting rework charge for each change.*

> *The program manager loaded the standards of the box build and booked the order. A standard called "other" was loaded at $25. For each unit shipped, the system recorded an "other" COST of $25. There was no correlating actual cost to offset it. If it "washed" in the bottom line, the $25 would end up as increased profits. Instead, it was taken as a "reserve" and held aside until the inevitable occurred—and it occurred without trashing the thin margin for the period.*

Here, the "other" cost is reserved for unplanned costs that are predicted to be against the customer work order. Although it all washes out in the bottom line—*Revenue minus Cost equals Profit*—the accounting for the details will ensure the right bottom line and specifically identify those costs that were and were not accounted for, as the gross margin line can rapidly erode when reporting.

Turn the Assets

Using those numbers from the P&L example, the inventory turns for the financial period were 0.9—not good. Turns are calculated as: material cost (sold), times 12 (this project's annual consumption), divided by the closing on-hand inventory balance, thus projecting the turnover annually.

Turning inventory is critical to cash flow and viability. In a hypothetical perfect world, we can provide the following to demonstrate the financial advantage of higher inventory turns:

Using the *70% of revenue is material cost* formula:

You have a $1M PO due at the end of a given month.
You order $700K of material to support the order.
The material comes in 30 days prior to the due date.
The material is released to the floor in week one of the month it is due.

Several shortages delay the start of the job 2 weeks.
During the last week of the month, as you build the product, you write checks for $700K (paying net 30 days to the suppliers).

The first week of the next month, you ship, one week late of the due date.

The customer sends you $1,000,000 thirty days later.

In this scenario, you had $700K of *your* cash (or maybe even the banks) out/tied up for 6 weeks.

Same situation, only . . .
You receive the material in the second week of the month that the order is due.

You turn the kit into product in one week and ship on the 25th.
You are paid net 30.

You are paid net 30: $1,000,000 on the 25th of the next month.

Five days later, you pay the suppliers (net 45.)

You held a million dollars for a few days and used no on-hand cash to fund the material in the order. The more aggressive you are on inventory, the less capital you have tied up in the payables and receivables cycle.

While the turns displayed above may seem unrealistic, the fact is that the lower your inventory turns, the larger the block of cash that is continuously needed to float the materials piece of the business.

Another boost to turning assets could be in the form of preferred terms.

A 2% discount for 10-day payments would bring the cash in early. You would be paid on the 5th and pay the suppliers on the 25th, holding the $700K for 20 days.

Sacrificing a couple of percentage points of profit may be attractive to the CM if the cash flow becomes stimulated.

To successfully turn inventory, the CM's core competencies must all be firing on all cylinders. First, the program/account manager must carefully negotiate and receive the order with enough lead time so that materials availability must not impact the schedule; this data comes from proper execution of the quote. Next, the ERP/MRP system must net out the requirements (read: be accurate), and the materials group must have all parts sourced properly and timely; this flows on down and ultimately the cycle time through the factory and proper workmanship will result in expediting the resultant invoice to the customer.

Now, take a look at the model and imagine that lines of credit are used to fund materials, multiple programs of high material content are in play, 80% of your customers are telecoms, and its 2001. When the CM's orders are put on hold because the OEM'S inventory is skyrocketing, the EMS company's cash flow stops, leaving their available assets tied up in material and work in progress, which is for the moment worthless, and the inbound material is betting on revenue from the work in progress to pay back the bank. When it all stops suddenly, it ain't pretty.

Note that the job shop companies slide the inventory model to the left and lower their risks in cash flow and make larger profits on labor and process efficiencies. This model, while not business critical, demonstrates that the 30% of the job shop material content can be managed to optimize cash flow and increase profits on investment dollar. It could be argued however, that the job shop has sufficient profits and would rather have material on hand and be able to execute on an opportunity, as the investments are nor that large or risky. Also, the material is standard stock, and will most likely be consumed by other, if not, eventual orders.

Excess or slow moving inventory is a turn killer. Residual inventory from older programs sits on the books with no forecasted consumption and negatively affects the asset turn formula. If the inventory can't be returned or sold, it must be written off (down) and hits the bottom line as a loss (or removed from the books).

Another turn killer is new product introduction. When a new product of low of moderate volume is launched, in addition to the start up inefficiencies are the minimum purchase quantities. As mentioned earlier, items can be packaged in the thousands. Add many product launches to the scenario, and a company can be literally put out of business because of too much sales—the cash to start the programs exceeding the revenue.

One of the more fundamentally backward practices is in the way materials are scheduled by EMS providers. When orders are entered, parts are planned to support the purchase order date, regardless of the availability of 100% of the parts. If a million dollars' worth of product is scheduled to be built 12 weeks out, then the materials to support that are piped and brought in regardless of the fact that a couple of parts have 16- and 20-week lead time. While this is often reviewed at the quote phase, stock positions and market changes often occur between the quote and order. Even when these issues are identified, the battle cry is to expedite, not reschedule the bulk of material to match the long lead items. That would be to admit defeat! The customer needs the product and a "make it happen" mentality kicks in. Often the battle is won, but when it is not, the cash flow is clobbered.

In addition to turning the inventory, asset utilization is a key metric. Idle machines are a bad thing.

Asset turns are *Net Income divided by Average Available Assets.*

For a manufacturing company, this number will be lower than the number at, say, a software company or a telemarketing firm. The equipment required to create revenue far exceeds that of the other industries. On the other hand, there is no R&D for a contact manufacturer.

The ultimate enabler of all good variances is revenue. The more shipped, the more absorption of indirect costs and overheads, and also the higher the inventory and asset turns. And of course, more gross profit dollars. Knowing this, some pretty interesting tactics have been employed, which only solve a problem in the very, very short term, yet seem irresistible when your back is against the wall at the end of the quarter or year.

"Invoice everything post wave!" was the command from a plant manager at SCI (circa 1990), with only a few hours remaining in the month (post wave is where the majority of the components are soldered to the circuit boards, leaving some final mechanical components and test to finish the manufacturing process).

First, there is a question of legality. This was a publicly held company and revenue was being claimed for product that had not shipped. Besides potential jail time, this created another risk. The next month, the factory must finish building the product and ship it without realizing any revenue, but spend the dollars to finish the job. So, a falsely inflated end of the month will show an upside in revenues—without their respective costs, resulting in higher net margins—and a major hole to dig out of the next day when they return to work. Also, there is now a problem with the order management system, as orders are shown as shipped to customers, yet they don't have the goods. This may result in a "special" list that is closely held by those with a need to know, until the factory is caught up. At another EMS company, this almost monthly list was nicknamed the "Pre-ship list," and was distributed to the account managers so they would not tell the customers the product was on the way.

The final impact of this activity is the fact that the customers are not going to pay—and pay at the agreed terms—until they receive the product. Asset turns take another hit, as these invoices are not paid on time and cash flow slows.

We have also heard the stories of "very slow trucks" *delivering* mountains of product early to customers, only to have it returned for credit a couple of weeks later, then reshipped on the scheduled date. Sometimes the trucks carried empty boxes!

Another tactic to bolster financial performance is to have inventory at the lowest number possible at the financial close. In addition to tenaciously scheduling materials for the period's close, often receiving docks would close early—refusing any and all inbound material regardless of terms. Finally, how about a nice million dollar plus return of material (and debit memo) to a supplier tagged as "defective" goods? This shipment need not be unpacked, as it will be determined to be OK and accepted back—early in the new financial period.

There are many stories and players in these games, both at the CM and OEM level, all of which happened a long time ago, well beyond any legal statute, and of course, have never happened since...

11. HBO

This chapter almost need not be written, as we have touched upon the impact of **human behavior in organizations** throughout this study. As keynoted in the "Dilemma" chapter, it is the behavior of people that often creates the irony in what would appear to be a straightforward solution to a given situation and the actual actions that are taken. It is also the reason why many *Best in Class* initiatives fail. It's not because the initiative was flawed or the company was not the right fit for such a program, but rather that the staff made it fail. This may boil down to an individual in the organization who, for whatever reason, has decided that he or she does not want to implement a new policy, strategy, procedure, or systemic tool to improve the performance of the business.

This type of individual can exist at a CM or OEM (as well as any other organization, for that matter), and the impact to the enterprise can be huge. Further adding to the irony is that this type of individual does not lurk in the background like a saboteur, but is well known, often confrontational, and often feared by other staff members. Yet management does nothing about it. Are they blind to it? Often, we believe they are. While they may see certain tensions within the staff, they also see the numbers being achieved in the *Goals and Objectives* department. Once again, the goals put on the staff may be counterproductive to the overall mission of the company and the performance on the staff as a whole.

> Earlier, we discussed the purchasing manager at the Massachusetts EMS company renegotiating with the supply chain in the quest for PPV, putting new product introduction at risk and increasing cycle times. Adding to the dilemma, new software was introduced to accelerate bid cycle times, automate data interchange with the supply chain, and provide a host of tools for supply chain analysis and new product introduction.

> *The problem was that this software was chosen by another department and was forced upon Purchasing. Strike three. There was just no way in hell this was going to fly. If used properly, the software would establish the standards for new products' material content via the bidding process and also provide supply chain information (like the engineer did) for the new product introduction cycle. But the PPV would be zero. Add to that the fact that the software was not a Purchasing initiative. The supply chain was tortured. Business was being won using the automated software and the suppliers received "scorecards" showing their winning performance. But no purchase orders materialized. On the execution side, the purchasing group re-bid everything (via fax!) to beat a couple of points out of the quote and award the business elsewhere. The results were poor performance, lost business, and a frustrated supply chain that became less responsive—hoping other CMs would win the business, as they could be dealt with. But, at the internal quarterly business review, upper management saw that Purchasing hit their PPV objective. On the Sales and Revenue side of the house, however...*

As we mentioned at the outset of this study, human resources are a variable, not only in performance, but also in behavior. Not until the human resource is on board is there a way to know how well he or she will perform or behave, unless there are good references or a history with the individual doing the hiring. Virtually all organizations, large and small, have some form of internal human behavior that impacts the overall mission of the company, impacts the daily operations, or, at a minimum, negatively affects the work environment (read: adds unneeded stress) and the performance of the other human resources that reside within it.

A basic internal conflict often seen in contract manufacturing is between Sales and Operations. Sales is the voice of the customer, often demanding the unreasonable at the wrong time, and highlights the business risks if the operations team does not pull through. Operations is constantly dealing with all of the variables associated with the customers and trying to ensure everything runs as smoothly (and profitably) as possible, so there is a constant push back on the sales team for relief.

So, while we can study behavior in these organizations and the things that drive it, we cannot predict it with any certainty. At this point is this study, however, the reader should have a good understanding of how people in organizations can behave and should be able to recognize certain behaviors and their source of motivation.

One basic assumption that can be made is that ***"compensation dictates behavior."*** Even with a level-headed playing field of reasonable, talented people, the basis by which you pay them will affect the way they behave. If you pay someone to renegotiate material costs, they may miss the objective of a smooth product launch. If your Quality department will get a bonus on creating dock-to-stock programs in a given time frame, be prepared for defect issues, as the program may have been forced to happen too quickly.

Human behavior inside contract manufacturing organizations can also be influenced by a change in the overall condition of the business operation. If a company has slowed down or been acquired, there may be fear of the loss of one's job. This may cause a department or manager to lash out at others, take credit, or build "walls" in the organization. Additionally, opportunities for personal advancement, or an overwhelming work situation can also drive people to similar behavior.

As highlighted throughout this study, the contract manufacturing company and its customers often engage in an adverse environment, creating conflict, thus putting the CM continuously on the defense. EMS providers differ from the job shops in that they have a very interactive relationship with the customer. Also, with the job shops we see more customers that do not have any expertise in the purchased service, and the relationship is much more of a hands off, "build to print," scenario. The EMS company, on the other hand, must continually align their supply chain with the components specified by the customer and resolve issues in specifications, availability, and price as an ongoing way of doing business.

12. Inside the OEM

While this study focuses on the contract manufacturers, a brief look at the OEMs they service is warranted. They come in many sizes, shapes, technologies, and personalities and are what drives the CM to success, if not completely out of their minds.

From a guy or gal with a new widget, to a multi-billion dollar aerospace company, these entrepreneurs and companies all engage in outsourcing of their manufacturing at some level. The smaller OEMs will have a limited staff, if any. Here the relationship can be very tight, as the principles of the company are involved directly with the manufacturer. For the CM, the risks are high, as the small OEM can easily fail and not meet their financial commitments to the CM.

In the mid-size to large OEM, we find a full infrastructure of systems and functional departments. These OEMs have preexisting revenue streams, a market presence, and experience at bringing products to market. In the largest OEMs we find new product teams with support from multiple skill sets: Engineering, Marketing, Materials, all working to bring products to market. Once launched, there may be a second group than manages the pipeline, forecasting, releasing, scheduling, and managing design changes throughout the products' lifecycle. Product Lifecycle Management (PLM) is a market sector for software companies. These products run parallel to the MRP, managing the configuration of products and the internal design and design maintenance efforts.

In a 2007 survey by Arena Solutions of 150 mid-market manufacturers, less than 10% were satisfied with their internal systems to manage new product development and introduction.

2007- Arena Collaborative Study, 04/01/07, Arena Solutions

The above survey shows the first challenge an OEM faces. They must be set up to succeed internally if they are to have a chance at succeeding externally. Additionally, the OEM faces many of the same objectives as the CM does, in financial, business process, and manufacturing process performance.

Business Models

Start up companies pose a higher risk to CMs in that they do not have a revenue stream to pay for the goods they order. Typically, start ups are funded by venture capital companies. The start up receives their funding in "rounds" and is on a timeline to get to market. If they track to the timeline, they get the next round, and, at some point, create enough revenue to stand on their own. If they do not hit the timeline, the next round of funding is subject to new terms, often surrendering more equity for the next cash infusion. In this phase in the life of an OEM, the OOC date is the most important metric.

Once off the ground with the wheels up, the OEM poses less of a risk to the CM. They also become a more desirable customer to the rest of the playing field.

The largest OEMs may choose to outsource none, some, or all of their manufacturing. Cell phone manufacturers build the majority of their product in house, yet outsource some. This model is attractive in that the most repeatable, efficient and predictable business can run at full efficiency in house—maximizing profits—while the less efficient, variable business can be offloaded, making the CM absorb the less than perfect efficiencies and schedule fluctuations.

The outsourcing strategies of the OEM will vary based on their products and their business plan. They may be forced to outsource a process that they could never master, such as dip brazing. Or, the

OEM may elect to outsource manufacturing, choosing between either a consignment strategy or a turnkey one.

Core Competence

As with the business models, the core competence list mirrors the CM's. But there is also: **Product Design, Product Marketing, and Logistics** (Logistics can be outsourced to a CM in a virtual factory scenario). The list, in total, emphasizes different competencies. Final assembly and test of a router, for example, may focus more on cycle time reduction, as the subassemblies have been fully tested and the product yields are almost guaranteed. **Materials management**, as mentioned earlier, becomes a strong suit as the OEM grows. Internal teams benchmark designs and production products, often working directly with EMS companies to ensure the component level materials are being bought at the best available price. Often, with the larger OEMs, the component manufacturer's sales team works with the OEM to be "designed in" and offers special pricing. This is known as a "registered" price, and is typically at a discount. The registration is then pointed to a distributor, who may have worked the deal (we now say, "opportunity") with the factory rep. In addition to registered components, special pricing may be obtained by the OEM if their (indirect) power is large enough to warrant a discount. The materials specialist at the OEM must manage this information down to the supply chain, often to multiple CMs purchasing the same components. The Materials group must then bring all the information they provide, plus the CM's input, and analyze and negotiate some very large manufacturing agreements when outsourcing to an EMS provider.

At the assembly level, proper balance between revenue and inventory is paramount, as the products coming in the door are at tremendous value. The build plan and the actual order flow are closely watched, especially at year end.

Financial Models

The OEM follows financial models similar to those used by the CM. They set their material standards at the assembly level, and may do final integration, configuration, and test in house, thus having variance monitoring similar to that of the CM. Their inventory turns are managed as well, especially with an outsourcing program to the EMS industry, where very high dollar items hit their dock to be configured into the final ship level products. Gross profit margins for the OEM are much larger than that of the CM, but they must fund the overhead of product development and marketing.

As mentioned above, start ups are on a timeline to revenue, set by their financial backers. Early on, the OEM is not concerned about the above model, but rather their getting products to market and creating revenue. Funding is typically in several rounds, with specific milestones. If they miss, the next round comes with pain. If they don't get the revenue stream up and stand on their own, an additional round of funding may cost much more—in equity—than the initial round. Unless the OOC day is near, the CM should not be affected by this, other than having an understanding for a sense of urgency by the start up.

HBO

The behaviors described in the CM chapters flow right into the OEM (some have been previously discussed). *Compensation dictates behavior, empire building*, etc., all make life at the OEM that much more fun. If anything, the OEM has even more of it than the CM. Remember the CM runs lean, and people just don't have much time for games. And, when push comes to shove, the CM can be the OEM's chew toy. Like a pawn, the CM will be sacrificed for another objective.

For some inexplicable reason, the OEMs protect their employees much more than the CMs do. Perhaps it's the extra lean approach to staffing that results in an HR department that does not embrace the employee. That is not to say that they are cruel or practice policies that are not ethical (domestically speaking).

The perception, as seen from the vantage point of the writer, is that the OEM, after identifying a bad apple in the bunch, must start a lengthy process to document the problem and provide the opportunity to correct it. Only after a certain time period where the problem is not remedied does the employee lose his or her job (unless the issue is severe, or violates the law).

In contract manufacturing, there is no patience for due process. Selective layoffs occur, as required, to eliminate the dead wood. Sometimes, The RIF total is one.

For those who are not on a probationary recovery plan, the real world personalities come through loud and clear.

Not so world-class?
The OEM executives that tout "CPIM" credentials and are self-proclaimed "supply chain optimization" experts fuel the fire...

In the desktop PC arena, one "player's" Top Gun negotiating team decided to consign an expensive microprocessor for their video card, lowering cost by eliminating the CM's 17% markup. A big cost savings was posted. While they continued their assault on cost, beating up the CM on "C" class hardware—negotiating to the tenth of a penny—they did not have the infrastructure to handle consigning the micro, and "gave away" six figures of product. True story.

The Materials group at the OEM may be measured on PPV as well, causing some of the other behavior mentioned earlier in this study. Often, inventory falls under the Materials group, as they are the ones executing the scheduling from their own ERP gyrations. While PPV objectives can cause some supply chain shifts resulting in risk and other costs to the OEM, the quest for a low inventory number at the quarter's close can result in some downright rude behavior.

We cited a real world example in the introduction of this study, where $30 million of inbound product was stopped, as the OEM had met their revenue goals and was now posturing the inventory to be as low as possible. Two suppliers were involved—the first had 3 million put on hold, as it was coming off the line.

"You shouldn't feel so bad; we are on our way to our other supplier to stop $25+ million..." The bottom line was if you wanted to be their supplier next year, you played ball with them.

Sometimes enough is enough...

A supplier of machined metal parts inked a contract with a Rhode Island OEM. The purchase order was for $130K for over 1000 units. After the first delivery, the OEM took no more. But the year's worth of parts had been run to achieve the price point. The OEM rescheduled the order out indefinitely. The vendor quickly sued and won $130K.

American Power Conversion, also of Rhode Island, instituted a program called "The Cost of Quality," whereby and rejection of materials resulted in fines to the supplier and a possible full credit for the parts. The fines were so severe, that, if enforced, they could mount to thousands of dollars for each occurrence. Some of the job shops, including a sheet metal shop with over a million a year at stake, refused purchase orders under the new terms.

Not all OEMs are evil. But if you are in the business of contract manufacturing, it is fun to share war stories on the ones that are—and these stories will typically boil down to the same set of customers (or individuals) in a given region or market.

It was once said, "On your best day you will be doing business with your friends. And on your worst day, you hope you are..." The OEM needs the CM, and often both staffs work hard, have fun, and make both parties successful building products. When dealing with the small start ups, these relationships are often enjoyed, as the primary point of contact will be a major equity player in the OEM, and the success of the CM's mission means everything to him or her.

13. Reasons to Outsource to a Contract Manufacturer

The decision to outsource some or all of the manufacturing of an OEM's products is sometimes made as the company is created; other times it is a decision made over time, because an internal manufacturing process is no longer efficient, does not have enough capacity, or does not fit the corporate objective.

Time to Market
Start up OEM companies need to get to market quickly with their products. Most often, this does not allow for the establishing of a manufacturing department to support production needs. Nor does this make financial sense so early on in the business cycle.

Start ups also pose the most risk to a contract manufacturer—some will not do business with them, i.e., Benchmark, whose target market consists of companies with at least $25 million in revenue. Often, a bond or LOC will be asked for, or even advance payment for materials and COD for the balance, if the customer has now credit history.

Cascade Communications, a venture-backed start up, awarded their business to SCI in 1995. SCI's asset manager declined terms and insisted on a 90-day LOC. This will cover 30 days of invoices, 30 days of WIP, and 30 days of material, in the event of a default. Based on the proposal, this amount would be $1.5 million. Cascade quickly complied, as their business plan included partnering with a major (top 5) EMS provider to not only successfully execute the manufacturing strategy, but also to lend credibility to the start up.

Capacity

Manufacturing companies may have seasonal spikes in demand, unpredicted increases, or may strategically plan in-house capacity to be less than forecasted demand to ensure high factory productivity and utilization. The outsourced capacity then handles the variable demand, while the factory runs linear.

Technical

Certain process steps, components, or subassemblies may require a skill or equipment that the OEM does not posses or may not have access to. Injection mold plastics require much more than a piece of equipment to be competent at producing production level parts, for example. Many of these technical requirements are the skills of the job shop arena. Also, the content of the final product may be much too small to warrant the capital investment and the acquiring of the skill sets to be competent and efficient in these areas. For example, take a small, custom machined part that makes up less than 10% of an electronic box build's cost. It makes more sense to focus engineering efforts on the electronics then on the skills required to make machined parts a consistent quality level.

Financial

As stated above, the machined part would require a significant capital investment as well, if produced in house. A simple cost analysis may find going to a subcontract scenario is just plain cheaper than building in house—including paying the subcontractor a reasonable profit over costs. Volumes may be too low to utilize assets properly, demand may be too uneven to have resources standing idle, or the overhead structure of the company may be too high due to location (real estate and wages).

The final destination/cost of transportation of the products may determine that outsourced manufacturing in the furthest away markets is a viable alternative to establishing global manufacturing. Large appliances are manufactured in Mexico for North American consumption, for example.

Also, when analyzing new products, the financial costs to support the manufacturing of them—be it increased capacity or new process infrastructure—may be too high to warrant capitalization.

Finally, there is the stabilization and predictability of costs. When making products in house, costs are variable. Each production run will shake out a different bottom line cost. To outsource and place an annual contract for the product or service makes this now a fixed cost—with no inefficiencies, no downtime, no strikes, and no bad news at the end of the financial period.

Core Competence

Are you a manufacturing company? This is the pitch the EMS companies give. Companies may be in the business of creating products, but are they the right choice to make them? Manufacturing the products you design may detract from your actual mission as a company with regard to time to market, market penetration, customer satisfaction/quality, and the ability to meet changing demand.

Will manufacturing be embraced, focused on, and funded as well as product development and marketing? If not, you are probably not a manufacturing company. If one were to look back at the financial performance of an EMS company, a less then well run manufacturing factory can easily cost more than the total costs proposed by the CM to build your products.

14. Fundamentals / DDFM

We hereby expand the three-letter acronym, DFM (Design for Manufacture), to a new, four-letter acronym, DDFM (Design Documentation for Manufacture).

DFM / DFT

The gifted engineer can create the next greatest thing. But, if he or she does not properly document the design, the odds of a successful introduction to manufacturing and market success grow thinner with each assumption and interpretation. Inconsistent or cumbersome documentation reduces efficiency (read: adds cost) and raises the risks to the OEM.

Thus, when a decision is made to outsource, there must be a conscious effort to consider the outside world when documenting designs, communicating specifications and requirements, and managing changes of the products that will be manufactured by third parties.

An "If it can be drawn, it can be built" mentality simply does not work in today's world of high tech manufacturing. Let's start with the design. In addition to Design for Manufacture, there is also Design for Test (DFT). The premise for both is to understand the manufacturing processes and validate products' designs so they will go through the processes as quickly, easily, and consistently as possible. Whether a sheet metal chassis, a cable assembly, a circuit board, or an MP3 player, the smoother it goes through the factory, the higher the yields, and as a result, the lower the costs. This will result in higher profits, or a lower price point to gain more market share. In addition to these benefits, there is a much simpler one: successful new product introduction. This statement will make perfectly clear sense after you have one fail.

Design for Manufacture brings the CM and the OEM to the table as true partners. The CM's and the OEM's engineering departments collaborate on product design requirements and the CM's manufacturing process limitations. In circuit board assembly, for example, the exact size of the PCB directly affects the cost of manufacture. First, the raw fab (blank circuit board) itself has sizes that are optimal, being created from larger, standard size panels of raw materials. Getting the most out of a panel reduces cost. Next, the size and shape of the circuit board may allow for better machine handling, or building multiple units at the same time by having the circuit boards in a panel that is later broken down into individual units in downstream manufacturing processes. When they would be broken down would also be studied. Manual processes are also considered in the design phase. Not only the less the better, but automation of component prep functions (small fixtures, etc.), and final assembly techniques, when considered at the front end of the design process, will have a huge payback at the back end of manufacturing and delivering products to market.

Test is a consideration that can really play into the creativity of the team working together, as both are variables during product development. Rather than designing a product that flows efficiently through a fixed piece of capital equipment, Functional Test (FCT) rigs can be configured to optimize process flow around the configuration of the product. And the products themselves can be designed to provide easy access for test. In one box build product cited in this study, the final test can be done with the product in its respective shipping containers. The test stand is PC- (laptop) based, and product deployed to the field can be re-tested prior to installation—without the labor and space requirements of unpacking them.

In the circuit board world, there is also In Circuit Test (ICT). This test is one where a dedicated, "bed of nails" type fixture is created and the circuit board is mounted to. A software program then "buzzes out" the board. The test station is a piece of capital equipment the EMS provider owns and maintains. The fixture and software are typically paid for by the customer as an NRE charge, and the costs for these can be in the tens of thousands of dollars, depending on the complexity of the board to be tested. ICT must be carefully planned during product development and implemented when the design is deemed production ready. Even when done right, the costs are significant to tool up a fixture and software for each circuit board in the OEM's portfolio of products. Typically, ICT is employed on complex, large circuit boards like a mother board, or like the ones we see in the telecom market. Smaller PCBs can be validated with quicker, less costly functional tests because they are easier to troubleshoot, due to their lower component count.

Design Documentation for Manufacturing / DDFM

The methods employed in documenting the product play just as critical a role in the success of manufacturing as the manufacturability of the design itself. Back in the Stone Age we had actual blueprints. They were large, blue, and smelled of the chemicals used to make them (hence the term, *Build to Print*). To quote a sheet metal chassis, the OEM's buyer would submit a request to engineering for documentation, receive several sets of blueprints, mail them to the respective bidders, and wait for the quotes to come in.

That has all changed. Not only are we now "real time" in communications, but the formats of the documentation enable quicker and better understanding of the requirements—if done right. From the component, on up through test and final pack-out, there are opportunities to be efficient, concise, and user friendly, all adding up to more efficient and accurate execution in manufacturing.

Part Numbers are the base identifiers of all things in product design and manufacturing. As products evolve into reality, there is a transition to a controlled environment (hopefully). Early on, product designs are loose, as the engineer needs flexibility and speed, not researching every part or relying on someone else to approve a change or control a spec. In addition to the engineering data about the part, the sourcing information for components becomes part of the specification. Catalogue parts are often specified with the catalogue's part number, not the manufacturer's specification. A fastener or washer may have a "Mouser" part number listed, or, a Panasonic capacitor may have a "Digi-Key" part number identifying it rather that the Panasonic part number. Mouser and Digi-Key are distributors of hardware and electronic components, not manufacturers. Using these catalogue numbers makes the engineer's job easier in research, ordering samples, and getting preliminary price data. At the point of transitioning to manufacturing, these part numbers often carry over to the manufacturing data as the approved manufacturer.

> To digress to some interchangeable Three Letter Acronyms:
> AML- Approved Manufacturers List
> AVL- Approved Vendor List
> QPL- Qualified Producers List
>
> While in their literal sense they take on slightly different meanings, for the most part, these TLAs are interchangeable in the industry and are the approved manufacturer and the specification or part number that they produce.

The above scenario does not appear to be a disaster, but it can cause one. The use of distributors' part numbers as the manufacturer's specification is rampant, and occurs daily throughout the industry. The distributor's part number can typically be crossed to the manufacturer (by other distributors) by merely looking it up. But if the part is ordered from the catalogue distributor, a nickel part can turn into an expensive nightmare.

In Digi-Key's catalogue, the same Panasonic capacitor may be listed under several Digi-Key part numbers: one for loose parts, when buying just a few for prototyping; one for a strip of parts from a reel when 50 to a few hundred are needed; and one for a full production reel of 3000 parts. The difference in pricing will be insignificant when compared to the impact the loose parts will have if they make their way to the factory floor.

Hypothetical
A 10 cent, 3 lead, surface mount inductor falls into the above category. A kit for 500 assemblies is in front of the auto-placement machine (called a chip shooter), which places parts at a quoted price of 7 cents each. There are 3 inductors per assembly and there are 1500 loose parts in the kit. The technician setting up the machine brings it to the attention of the production planner.

Options:
1. Tear down the set-up, reject the parts and cycle them back through Purchasing to order more of the same parts in the proper packaging (at this point, the reader's mind should start adding up the dollars). The rejected parts would have to be scrapped or repackaged by the CM to accommodate the equipment, because they were supplied correctly by the supplier. The proper parts would have to be purchased as an emergency buy and sent via overnight carrier and processed into the system. Once done, the kit would have to be rescheduled into the workflow, at best, a day or two behind schedule.

2. Leave the machine set up. Bring in the process engineer. Create a temporary work instruction to have the parts hand placed on the boards by a person as they come off the chip shooter and before they go into the re-flow oven (which solders the parts to the boards). This path results in some downtime to edit the machine to "skip" that part, as well as the human resource required to place the components manually. This, of course is not the best way to do this and there will be an expected decrease in quality, resulting in some additional labor for "touch up" and a possible reduction in test yield issues at the back end, all because a 10-cent part had the wrong callout on its AVL.

Getting the AVL right is not a difficult thing and can help make manufacturing run smoothly. Besides, we are talking about a Panasonic part, and should not be talking about the people who sell them (Digi-Key) when creating manufacturing ready documentation.

A white paper created by the author completes the dialogue on part numbers and the strategies one can employ when documenting products for manufacturing, both internally and externally.

white paper

part numbering schemes for electronic design and manufacturing

http://www.mfgit.com

Background

One of the pitfalls in electronics design is the idea that there is a perfect part numbering scheme and we can come up with it. And 73 digits later, it is done. Another strategy is to tie a part number or scheme to some number or standard external to the enterprise, which, when changed, modified, or abandoned, renders the scheme useless.

For creating unique part numbers, the options vary from 5- or 6-digit random numbers assigned in order as needed, to complex, hyphenated sequences with alphanumeric codes that tell you exactly what the part's specification is. You can argue it either way. For one enterprise, their chosen scheme is absolutely required for the way they do business. The next will have needs 180 degrees from this.

For contract manufacturers, the decision is whether to use their customer's part number, often with an identifying prefix, create an internal number, or use the manufacturer's part number. The prefix eliminates the rare chance of duplication from another customer. It also stacks the data in the database by customer and is thus user friendly.

Rule #1: Keep it simple. The more keystrokes, the greater the opportunity for error. The more complex the formula, the smaller the number of those who will understand it and use it.

What drives ERP/MRP in electronics manufacturing is the **Primary Part Number**. This is what identifies the assembly, the subassemblies, the components, and even the solder used to holding them all together.

Decisions on data structure determine the accuracy, flexibility and efficiency of the downstream processes in the enterprise, as these **Primary Part Numbers** move in huge volumes throughout the infrastructure.

The various part numbering schemes that exist throughout the electronics industry, include:

Manufacturer's part number
Distribution part number
EMS part number
OEM part number

The following review will consider each of these strategies for creating a Primary Part Number when designing a product.

Manufacturer's Part Number

Here is where you get some really "big" numbers and some really "small" ones. Their numbers are long for a reason, as there is a lot of intelligence built in. Also, part numbers for certain components can vary, based on packaging and other parameters, including new part numbers reflecting the latest mergers and acquisitions. The result is that you can have multiple part numbers for the same part (from one manufacturer). It is rumored that some part numbers identify the component and its special pricing for a given customer, making specification research challenging.

Manufacturer's part numbers can become very confusing. As a result, there are third party software companies dedicated to maintaining and providing an understanding of this infinite volume of data, such as IHS, Inc.

While a design may come together quickly using manufacturers' part numbers, the enterprise should be aware that the ease and concise manner of identifying parts this way initially has an opposite affect when the product is released to manufacturing.

When designing a product, consideration for manufacturers' part numbers should be as follows:

Using this number as a primary identifier is probably the most difficult scenario to keep accurate, maintain, and consistently execute on in ongoing manufacturing.

The field where the manufacturer's data will reside should allow for as many digits as possible.

Distribution Part Number

Some distributors have their own part numbering schemes, like Digi-Key. This resolves the above dilemma created when marketing many of the world's components. Of course, the manufacturers' part numbers have to reside "somewhere" in the system.

These schemes, however, vary from distributor to distributor and have created a need for even more cross referencing (i.e., an engineering BOM might have Digi-Key part numbers all over it, because that is how the prototype was built. For production volumes, the major distributors can cross reference these numbers to the manufacturer's number and their internal number as well).

When considering the distribution part number:

It can be treated as a "Manufacturer / MFG Part Number" in the Approved Vendor List, without creating a separate cross reference table—the distributors can cross from each other.

EMS Provider's Part Number

In the food chain, the EMS provider is at the bottom. The decision on how data will be formatted is made at the OEM (a different format from every OEM) and the EMS provider has to handle them all in their day-to-day business.

So we will address the EMS provider first, in hopes of building a "conscience" when creating the OEM part numbers. This conscience might be appreciated in the OEM's manufacturing department, or at your EMS provider, if you are outsourcing your product's manufacturing.

There are choices an EMS provider faces when structuring Primary Part Numbers in their ERP:

Use the Customer's Part Numbers
Use the Manufacturer's Part Number
Create Internal Part Numbers
One Internal Part Number for each manufacturer's part number
Internal Part Numbers as needed

Option: Use the Customer's Part Numbers

This strategy is most common amongst the largest EMS providers. In most cases, **a prefix is assigned** to the part number to eliminate the possibility of duplicates from another customer and also to align data *by customer* for sorting and searching.

What's Good:

The customer's part masters and AVLs are directly loaded and maintained in the EMS provider's ERP system.

When communicating and sharing data with customers, the component's data is in "their language."

When a strategic buy or registered price comes into play, the components are segregated for that customer's use.

Inventory positions and liabilities are created solely on the activity of that specific customer.

Limited resources are required for part number management and creation.

Works well in a focused factory environment where there are only a few customers being considered.

What's Not So Good:
Multiple (customer) data formats must be loaded.

Any "intelligence" in the customer part numbering scheme is typically lost.

The same components will be stocked in separate locations for each customer that specifies it.

The same part will be bought multiple times as separate ERP "events." This compounds the transactions required to process the parts through the enterprise. You can actually be expediting and canceling/returning the same component at the same time!

Total, company-wide usage of the component may not be leveraged for best pricing.

Excess positions can be unnecessarily created, when another customer's demand could have consumed the overage.

Sometimes, customers don't have part numbers!

Clearly, there are trade-offs. The larger EMS providers can afford the cost and overhead of multiple purchases for the same part. On multi-million dollar programs it is most important to have the inventory segregated, at the agreed levels, with any special pricing

remaining specific to that inventory/customer bucket. Top-level customer contracts can define inventory liability and the potential surplus/duplication of parts is considered a carrying cost/overhead cost, as opposed to risk.

Option: Use the Manufacturer's Part Number

As stated earlier in this brief, using manufacturers' part numbers is probably the most difficult scenario for the EMS provider (or the OEM for that matter) to structure and control.

What's Good:
The MFG part is easy to understand by all, especially in the procurement cycle.

Common (fewer) inventory locations.

Total volume purchase to maximize pricing advantage
Lowers excess exposure.

Streamlines overhead by reducing total part number count.

What's Not So Good:
Large swings in part number length and format.

The ability to have multiple manufacturers' part numbers for the same part, resulting from packaging (tape and reel) change in format, or manufacturer's acquisition (this can result in issues at incoming inspection).

The inability or extreme difficulty to have multiple sources for a customer's part (primary part number).

> *If AMP#1234 and Molex#5555 are on the AVL, which one do you structure?*
> *If you structure the Molex under the AMP as an acceptable alternate, a new customer may have "AMP only" on their AVL resulting in*

a risk to the integrity of the parts or the need to create a special part number and stocking location.

If used, the enterprise will be faced with primary part numbers ranging from a few to too many digits (it has been seen where the comments field or other data fields are used to complete tediously long numbers). These numbers must travel throughout the enterprise and are present on everything from invoices to stocking bins; process sheets; not to mention all MRP-related data. Also, the flexibility given via a multiple AVL scenario becomes very difficult to manage or take advantage of.

Option: Create Internal Part Numbers

Many mid-tier EMS providers go this route. The intent is to eliminate the confusion inherent in manufacturers' part numbers by standardizing the data field format. Customer formats can vary widely and cause data management issues as well. Also, using one base numbering system for the ERP, since each component is (in theory) bought once, stocked in one place, and so on, eliminates the multiple buy and bin dilemma of the "customer part number" scenario.

Two Approaches:

1. One Internal Part Number for each Manufacturer's Part Number:

What's Good:
This standardizes the part numbering scheme.

You will be dead nuts on with respect to excess inventory exposure and having the minimum amount of bins in your stock room.

What's Not So Good:
Has the same AVL issues as using a manufacturer's part number.

A customer AVL is needed as a reference document.

2. Internal Part Numbers as Required, with Multiple AVLs:

What's Good:
This approach eliminates the need (most of the time) for a customer AVL reference document.

As new part numbers are needed, Internal Part Numbers are created.

What's Not So Good:
Requires research for creating new part numbers and AVLs in the part master database

May not work as well as you thought . . .

Example: If an internal part number has AMP #1234 and Molex #55555, and a new customer only allows the Molex part, a new part number, stocking location, etc., must be established. Now there are duplicate parts in various bins—though it's not nearly as bad as the Customer Part Number scenario.

The difficulty the EMS provider faces is being able to consolidate demand for procurement and reduced material overhead, while maintaining the integrity of multiple customers' unique AVLs. Where a strategic buy is made, or special pricing is given, these parts must run outside of the normal inventory flow as well.

Settling on a part numbering strategy at an EMS provider is difficult, and there's a lot at stake. Sometimes, a combination of the above strategies will be used. For "C" class items, such as passive components, an internal part numbering system may be employed—in support of an in-house stocking program, for example. Customers may be forced to open up their AVL to accommodate this program, as the EMS provider's stocking partner typically favors certain manufacturers. For certain "A" items or custom parts requiring drawings to fabricate, the customer part number may be

used. And where a certain item is purchased the same exact way every time, like solder, packaging, or labels, a manufacturer's part number may be part of the internal number.

OEM Part Number (and EMS internal part number)

To create an electronic assembly, the process of creating documentation must serve two masters. The first is the designer (AKA Engineering). The second is the builder (AKA Manufacturing). While these two masters take on many identities (i.e., internal or external), their core needs are the same.

The **designers** create products and output data, including part numbers. Also, on an ongoing basis, they must maintain part number data and create new ones as required.

The **builders** use this data to procure components, manage work flow, create manufacturing processes, and reliably build the products.

There are many considerations:

How many digits will be used
AVL—how many suppliers, or generic specs if possible
How to format descriptions for searching for data
Industry specs
Government specs
Military specs
EAN-UCC specs
Cage codes
SIC codes
NEDA codes
Revision control
Lot code traceability
How new numbers will be assigned
How much intelligence will be in the number
General: digits, characters, descriptions
Multi-level needs
Subassemblies—will you build them stand alone?

And let's not forget about RoHS!

It all comes down to deciding if the primary part number will tell us **EXACTLY** what the item is, tell us **IN GENERAL** what the item is, or tell us **NOTHING** about what the item is.

The Primary Part Number's format provides the opportunity to group components and provide information regarding the item's specification. While it is possible to continue on and provide the balance of the specification in the scheme, the number will become confusingly long and varied in length.

A uniform, structured part number, in a reasonable length, that provides partial information and sorts data in a format that groups like components for research and materials management. The **description field,** if used properly, can augment this data and provide, in many cases, the balance of the specification.

If the part number can provide GENERAL information about the item, it will be easy to use, understand, and have a consistent format throughout the enterprise. A properly formatted description follows suit in aiding data management.

A Case for Part Number Standardization

Let's look back at all of the considerations for a component's specification.

If we are to create an intelligent part numbering scheme, **the Primary Part Number can only do so much.** The **description field, however,** is also universally required by ERP and Product Lifecycle Management (PLM) systems. So, in the quest to come up with the utopian part number, the description can help the cause. If treated properly, descriptions can be utilized to refine and complete an intelligent part numbering scheme.

As the Dewey Decimal System organizes the world's books, we can mimic its sorting capabilities and format with data to the left of the decimal, right of the decimal, and in the description field. The first decision: How many total digits will be allowed? When considering this, the question arises, is this: a) the maximum number, or b) the standard format that all parts will have?

The latter of the two makes best sense for data structuring.

When considering a global economy, the EAN-UCC specs come into play. They have a limit of **14 characters**, which seems like a lot, but we can quickly consume the digits when establishing an intelligent format. Also, when (or if) our conscience kicks in, we may remember our outsourcing partner and the need to add a prefix to the part number. This prefix will be needed for component labeling and bar coding.

Thus, a 12-digit/integer part number will provide the EMS provider with two alphanumeric digits to be added as a prefix, totaling 14.

Hyphens: Yes or No?

We prefer the hyphen to Dewey's Decimal for the following reasons:

The dot is typically too small, and can be missed or interpreted and/or entered as a comma. The dot also appears at the "bottom" and can be obliterated by a line or underline (thus, we also dislike underscores in part numbers).

The hyphen takes up valuable character space, so it should not be treated lightly. It does, however offer a significant visual enhancement to the part number. Also, a significant delineation can be established between "standard intelligence" and "variably intelligent" data.

If three of the 12 digits/integers were used for intelligent, macro categorization, followed by a hyphen, the remaining 8 integers could be used for random, or a mix of random and intelligent, information.

Save Space

One potential nuisance in part numbering is the use of spaces as delimeters. Enough said. Spaces do nothing but add confusion. When reciting the part number, the space may be a "pause" and misinterpreted. Keystroking the part numbers into various systems and databases, the same inconsistencies can create issues in later, downstream processes.

PROPOSITION "XXX-000000xx":

In this proposition the **first three digits are reserved for a standardized, intelligent format.** Three digits should satisfy most possibilities in manufacturing. The series starts at the highest numbers, the 900 series reserved for "Ship Level" products/assemblies. While there are 99 numbers here, there are virtually an infinite number of ship levels, when taking in the whole 12-digit, alphanumeric possibilities.

The top three – 900 – 800 – 700 series can be dedicated to segregating different families of products or top levels, such as spares, subsystems and different product lines. The next digits after the hyphen can be used for product identifiers in a high mix enterprise, and major component specification data.

900 – top-level assembly – ship level series

800 – second level series – ship level, modules and major custom items

700 – third level series – module/harness/subassembly

Next in the series is the "meat" of component configuration, which provides intelligence at the commodity level. Each level can be configured for specific commodities with 99 numeric digits (plus alpha) for categories.

600 – PCB series/flex circuits
500 – "A" item electronic components
400 – "B" item electronic components
300 – "C" item electronic components
200 – hardware, mechanical
100 – packaging, consumable, reference, non-inventory, service

Variable Intelligence:

The next six integers define the item. One's "conscience" should remember that others outside the enterprise will have to deal with these numbers, including the EMS provider and the components suppliers.

Declare, but don't restrict a pattern . . .

The left integers will describe the part and the right integers will be the unique identifiers for the component. This is not finite. If all six are needed for the unique identifier, they can be used. If all six are to be used to identify the spec, so be it. The general rule is: the intelligence starts at the left, and diminishes as the unique identifiers are needed.

If a unique item that is specific to a manufacturer's number makes sense, or a series of manufacturers' part numbers make sense, then the six digits can profile to that, say, a series of labels or models of power supplies. Just be cognizant of how they appear in data sorts and searches.

Examples:

A robotic company uses a ton of hardware in various materials. They need to spec in a ½ inch, 440 brass, hex head screw.

In the 200 series for hardware we have structured:

210 – fasteners
211 – nuts
212 – bolts
213 – screws
and so on . . .

213-B44001XG
B	= brass
44	= 440 series
001	= random/assigned identifier
X	= generic, open source
G	= RoHS compliant

The description field completes the remainder of the intelligence. The 999 unique (or more if alpha characters are used) are available for a 440 brass screw.

For this enterprise, the profiling of the material is more important than the size or head shape, thus all brass screws will be lumped together in the data sort and searches.

For electronics, the package is more important. A 50V 4700 *Uf*, 1206, ceramic capacitor is displayed below.

In the 300 series,

320 – capacitors
321 – smt 1206
322 – smt 0805
323 – smt 0603
324 – smt 1401
325 – smt 0201
326 – tbd
327 – tbd
328 – PTH Axial
329 – PTH – radial

325-50V001RG

50V = voltage designation
001 = unique identifier, (or MFG code for CM internal)
X = generic part/open AVL
R = restricted AVL
M = multi AVL
G = lead free *(green)*

The remaining two integers have been filled with optional information: mil spec part vs. commercial; and the all-important "lead free" designation. For custom parts, fabs, metal, etc., the last two integers can be used for the drawing revision.

LEVERAGING DESCRIPTIONS

If formatted properly, the description field completes the intelligence of the primary part number. When sorting and scanning the descriptions, if consistent, descriptions provide data that cannot be properly displayed in six digits.

Examples
The screw's description would be formatted as follows:
Screw,brass,440,0.50L,hex

As with the part number, the standardized intelligence lives at the left side and works its way to the right. Variable descriptors live toward the right in the equation. The commas, if used, need to be consistent throughout the part numbering scheme.

The positioning of the reflective data—that data which echoes the intelligence in the part number will provide a clean, visual affect when scanning the data. This will assist in locating existing or creating new part numbers.

213-B44001XG   Screw,BRASS,440,0.50L,hex
213-B44002XG   Screw,BRASS,440,0.25LPH

213-B44003XG   Screw,BRASS,440,1.25L,hex
213-S22006XG   Screw,SS,220,1.0L,Hex

The capacitor would also have a description that would allow easy look up and provide the balance of the intelligence: The resulting part could be "bought to description," because enough data is present.

321-50V47MMG Cap,1206,50V,4700uf,5%
322-50V1M0MG Cap,120650V,1000uf,1%
322-10V047XG Cap,0805,10V,47uf,1%

When creating a new part number for a 50 volt part, the scan for a preexisting component would bring the specialist to the data sort where all of the 50 volt caps "live," and the data must be scanned, because of its more random nature. The layout of the description should facilitate a relatively painless final level search (999 unique total scan). The data in the description field typically provides enough information for the part to be procured.

The description field's size should be large, between 30 and 40 integers. At some point, no mater how large the field, there will be a component whose vital information exceeds the spaces provided. This is just a fact of life and each enterprise will deal with it in its own way.

BOM Tree Example

900 – PK400006	Ship, Widget, 4000 series, UK
800 – PK400006	Tested, Widget, 4000 series
700 – PK40000006	PCBA, Tested, 4000 series
600-PK48880C	PCB, 14 layer,
321-50V001MF	Cap,1206,50V,4700uf,5%
321-50V005MF	Cap,120650V,1000uf,1%
322-10V012CF	Cap,0805,10V,47uf,1%
213-B4400100	Screw,brass,440,0.50L,hex
213-B4400200	Screw,brass,440, 0.25LPH
213-B4400700	Screw,brass,440, 1.25L,hex
213-S2200600	Screw,SSteel,220,1.0L,Hex

Part Master Schema Example

900 – top-level assembly – ship level series
800 – second level series – ship level, major subassembly, purchased modules, subassemblies major subcontract items.
890-XXXXXXxx Ship sub assy
880-XXXXXXxx Ship, sub assy
870-XXXXXXxx Major modules, subsystems
860-XXXXXXxx Purchased modules, standard
850-XXXXXXxx Power supplies, converters, inverters
840-XXXXXXxx Custom, electronics
830-XXXXXXxx Fabrication, electro mechanical
820-XXXXXXxx Fabrication, metal
821-XXXXXXxx Sheet metal
824-XXXXXXxx Stampings
825-XXXXXXxx Machined
829-XXXXXXxx Welded, brazed
810-XXXXXXxx Fabrication, plastic
800-XXXXXXxx Other

700- third level series – PCB assembly level /Sub Assemblies
700-XXXXXXxx PCBA, *(model reference)*
710-XXXXXXxx DAU, *(model reference)*
750-XXXXXXxx FLEXASSY, *(model reference)*
770-XXXXXXxx Cable Assy

600- PCB series / Flex circuits
600-XXXXXXxx PCB, LYR, *(top-level reference)*
650-XXXXXXxx FLEX, *(material), (top-level reference)*

500- "A" item Electronic components
500-XXXXXXxx Strategic, custom component – chip, chip set
510-XXXXXXxx Strategic, custom component – other
520-XXXXXXxx Microprocessor, IC, chip set
530-XXXXXXxx IC,—————-
537-XXXXXXxx IC, PTH,…….

540-XXXXXXxx
550-XXXXXXxx CONX (large connectors)

400- "B" item Electronic components
410-XXXXXXxx
420-XXXXXXxx
430-XXXXXXxx switches, relays
440-XXXXXXxx
450-XXXXXXxx
460-XXXXXXxx
470-XXXXXXxx connectors
471-XXXXXXxx header, pins
472-XXXXXXxx corresponding terminals

300- "C" item Electronic components
300- Resistors *Description Format*
301-XXXXXXxx Res, 1206,——ohm,—%,—w,
302-XXXXXXxx Res, 0805,——ohm,—%,—w,
303-XXXXXXxx Res, 0603,——ohm,—%,—w,
304-XXXXXXxx Res, 0401,——ohm,—%,—w,
305-XXXXXXxx Res, 0201,——ohm,—%,—w,
306-XXXXXXxx TBD
307-XXXXXXxx TBD
308-XXXXXXxx Res, Axial,——ohm,—%,—w
309-XXXXXXxx Res, Radial,——ohm,—%,—w
310- Resistor network
311-XXXXXXxx Res, Ntwrk,
320- Capacitor *Description Format*
321-XXXXXXxx Cap, 1206,—-V,——uf,—%
322-XXXXXXxx Cap, 0805,—-V,——uf,—%
323-XXXXXXxx Cap, 0603,—-V,——uf,—%
324-XXXXXXxx Cap, 0401,—-V,——uf,—%
325-XXXXXXxx Cap, 0201,—-V,——uf,—%
326-XXXXXXxx TBD
327-XXXXXXxx TBD
328-XXXXXXxx Cap,Axial,—-V,——uf,—%

329-XXXXXXxx Cap,Radial,—-V,——uf,—%

330- Ferrite
331- Axial
332-
333-
340- Diode, LED
345- LED
350- Transistor
360-
370-
380-

200- Hardware, Mechanical
210-XXXXXXxx *(fasteners)*
211-XXXXXXxx *nut, (material), (thread), (size)*
212-XXXXXXxx *Bolt, (material), (thread), (size), (head)*
213-XXXXXXxx *Screw, (material), (thread), (size), (head)*
214-XXXXXXxx *Washer, (material), (ID), (OD), (lock? split? flat?)*
215-XXXXXXxx Rivet,
216 XXXXXXxx Press-fit
220-XXXXXXxx *(terminal blocks, standoffs)*
230-XXXXXXxx Magnetics
240-XXXXXXxx
250-XXXXXXxx grommets, bulkheads
260-XXXXXXxx
270-XXXXXXxx Wire, cable
271-XXXXXXxx Tubing
272-XXXXXXxx Heat shrink
273-XXXXXXxx Terminals, lugs
274-XXXXXXxx
275-XXXXXXxx
280-XXXXXXxx

100- Packaging, Consumable, Documentation, Software, NON-MFG, Reference

SUMMARY

No part numbering scheme is perfect. The more information (longer) in the part number, the greater the risk of mistakes that can occur with data entry. Attempts to use external data, such as manufacturers' part numbers creates variable formats and restricts flexibility when considering the AVL.

Using an internal part numbering system, whether an OEM or a CM, provides the opportunity to inject a level of intelligence that will be beneficial to all handling the data, while keeping the part numbers' length to a minimum. The description field, if treated properly, can complete the intelligence, and often provide enough information to accurately procure the component. The CM's challenge is to handle many OEM customers while maximizing inventory turns and maintaining integrity in the customer AVL. If the CM handles many of these formats with different prefixes, there would be consistency in the way data is sorted, and the description could be relied upon to complete the intelligence.

In a utopian world, the first three integers would be a world wide industry standard. With recommended formats for the six digits, but allowing the enterprise the freedom to use the integers it deems best. The last two digits allow for revision control of fabricated items and the ability to address the impending lead free requirements.

The total of 11 integers (plus hyphen) is not many. But in the electronics industry, this should be enough (for example, you can have 999, 50 volt 1206 capacitors). If not, a simple deployment of alpha characters can expand the capacity exponentially.

The higher conscience in this scheme will be appreciated in your manufacturing department (internal or external), as well as those who handle and view these primary identifiers on a daily business, right on down to the accounts payable department.

www.mfgit.com

BOM Structure is touched upon in the white paper on Part Numbering Schemes. Simple, organized Bills of Materials (BOM) are not difficult to create or maintain. It is a tedious and sometimes complicated endeavor, however. The interdependency of components and their product structures can create a nightmare in maintenance. A worse nightmare occurs when they are not maintained. Again, this is not difficult, just tedious. A methodical eye for detail is required, with a strong, steadfast process for change control.

A bill of material may be in a single level, "flat" format, or an "indented", multi-level format. A flat, or single level bill of material, is a list of parts that make up one assembly. The structure will have each component's identifying part number, the description, and the quantity of each item, as a minimum requirement. Depending on industry there can also be: Unit of Measure, Revision, Sequence Number, AVL, and, for PCB assemblies, Reference Designators (identifying the location of the components on the board).

Data non-essential to documenting the product's design, but of significant value can include purchasing information and other product descriptors, such as tolerances, shapes and sizes, obsolescence, or lifecycle information.

Many BOMs are created in a spreadsheet, or exported from engineering software to a spreadsheet. All BOMs should be able to be provided in a spreadsheet format.

In cases of **multiple AVL options**, the additional data can be displayed in additional columns: **"Manufacturer Name | Manufacturer PN | Manufacturer 2 Name | Manufacturer 2 PN,"** or in a vertical representation, with the primary part number repeating or blank spaces occurring until a new primary part number appears.

Multi-level bills of materials add a few more critical points of data. First, there are subassemblies reporting to the higher level subassemblies and the top-level assembly. These are identified by part numbers, but must be coded as an assembly, rather than a part. Also their relationship to the next higher level must be established. For example, if a pair of stereo speakers makes one final, ship level product, the parts for each speaker will be on the same level of the indented structure, so we must know which parts report to the left speaker and which ones report to the right.

While CAD solutions help engineers design things, PLM (Product Lifecycle Management) solutions aid in the documentation of components, product structures and their evolution, on through end of life. In addition to BOM structures, there are also internal project management progress monitoring tools, and change management controls.

Often, BOMs or Parts Lists are present on the drawing. This keeps the engineering drawing and the bill of material on the same document and under the same revision. This is commonly found on metal fabrication and cable assembly documentation, as the lists are typically small.

Technical Specifications and Formats

Technical specifications include the above parts and structures, plus all related media to produce a given product. This data package can also include: mechanical drawings, manufacturers' data sheets, test specifications/procedures, schematics (for electronic designs), special work instructions, rework instructions (typically an ECO), and PCB fabrication data (called Gerber files).

When a product is made in house, or at a CM for many years, the documentation may not reflect exactly what is going on. Over time, changes, fixes, and "tweaks" to the manufacturing process and configuration are made, and may go undocumented. In the industry, this is known as "tribal knowledge," and it can really bite you in the rear if you attempt to move manufacturing out of house or change CMs. Over longer periods of time, the staff changes and those who knew the intimate details of the products are now gone. The remaining staff knows what to buy and how to assemble it, but not why. These people are the only way the product can be successfully built without a major engineering effort to re-document and qualify the products.

Specifications come in many formats. As we mentioned earlier, we started with blueprints. We have since evolved to electronic media, of which, the majority is an output from some software program—be it a CAD system or MRP export of a product's structure. Often, we see PDF files and Text files with pertinent data. The PDF files are excellent for things with pictures or mechanical drawings. For more mechanically intensive things, CAD drawings are used, such as for a sheet metal housing, or machined part.

Within these formats are the materials requirements. The list of materials can be present on the drawing or in a separate file. As we migrate to the electronics industry, the Parts Lists/BOMs are almost always on a separate list. As we detailed the structure of part numbers and bills of material, the format in which the data is received is equally important.

Rule: An Excel spreadsheet is the only format in which to provide a bill of material to another party.

If only this were true in real life. Additionally, each piece of data, as depicted above, must be placed in individual cells in the spreadsheet.

Excel is the "Lazy Susan" of software applications. Most applications can export to it, and many can import from it. And every person involved in the value chain knows how to use Excel; for handling and analyzing bills of materials, Excel is used throughout the industry. Additionally, the major component distributors work best with Excel. They use automated software to quote components and can import from, and export back to, Excel spreadsheets. Of note, the distributors' software analyzes the manufacturer's name and the part number. If the two are present in the same cell, the software will not work and the bid must be done manually. If you are an electronics designer, and there is one only thing you will take away from this chapter- this must be it.

The use of Excel as defined will increase speed, efficiency, and accuracy in the downstream manufacturing processes of data management and supply chain execution. If a bill of material is supplied on a .DWG file, TXT file or PDF file, the first step in the process will be to convert it to Excel, adding keystrokes, which takes time and increases the opportunity for error.

More real life:
An EMS company receives a bid package for four circuit board assemblies. All of the files are in a PDF format. The BOMs are not in the best shape; there are some missing specifications; and most of the parts' specifications that are present are catalogue numbers from a European distributor. Furthermore, there are no primary part numbers for the components, just descriptions.

The cycle time for this bid should be less than two weeks, including one full week for the supply chain to respond to the component requests. The actual "hands on" time for a quote of this magnitude should be in the 6-8 hour range.

Initially it is a "No-Bid," due to incomplete documentation. But the EMS company does not want to pass on the opportunity, so they hire a third party company (Ora Technology) that specializes in proposal management to work the bid. First, the BOMs must be restructured in Excel and a primary part number library is created to identify common components across the four assemblies. Then, the components themselves must be reviewed and matched up to manufacturer's specifications—not the obscure distributor's. The bid takes five weeks to complete and there are over 70 billable hours. The proposal is submitted as "budgetary," due to assumptions that had to be made, as well as several components without pricing listed as "No-Bid" due to insufficient information.

The above example demonstrates the benefit of having an "industry friendly" documentation package before stepping outside of the OEM. The OEM is now behind schedule in the outsourcing of their products and, even though they may be able to make a sourcing decision, the final costs are not yet known and there is much work to be done before a purchase order can be accepted by the EMS provider to start the manufacturing cycle.

Technical and Quality Requirements

When designing a product that will enter the market, one must consider any requirements that may be placed on the product or the manufacturing of the product in order for it to be "approved" in the market. A UL approval, for example gives electronic devices a safety approval. In order to maintain this approval (after the product is qualified), a file must be maintained by the manufacturer, and periodic on site audits occur to ensure the approved design and manufacturing methods have not changed. TUV and CSA are other UL-like private enterprises that will approve and offer credibility via a label on individual products.

Manufacturing facilities may also be certified to make products for a specific industry. Department of Defense work will impose military specifications for inspection. For example, MIL-I-45208 would be reviewed for compliance at a supplier via a site visit by the OEM's quality representative.

FDA, FAA, AS9000, all certify the manufacturing facility to a level of quality rather than the products that are made in them. Perhaps the most well known is the ISO9000 certification which swept the world in the 90s and continues today. The three manufacturing certifications are 9003, for repair, 9002 for manufacturing, and 9001 for design and manufacturing. ISO also covers the medical arena with ISO13485, though FDA regulation also must be considered.

Over time, the ISO certification has replaced some of the military standards, like 45208. ISO 9000 is more of a process control certification rather than setting quality standards. If implemented, there will be a set of procedures that the company states it will follow. There will be evidence of employee training, evidence that it is followed, and evidence that there are internal audits monitoring the system.

Workmanship itself has another set of standards. For electronics, there is IPC. IPC-610 is the most touted standard that is adhered to in the EMS arena. These standards set the level of acceptable workmanship of the repeatable processes outlined in ISO.

The latest standard being imposed is RoHS. The Restriction of Hazardous Substances Act eliminated certain contaminants from the manufacturing of electronics, namely lead. Solder had to be lead free, resulting in an overhaul of the soldering process for nearly every EMS provider on the planet.

Change / Rev Control

When things change, so must the documents that define them.

One of the dilemmas in documentation control (AKA configuration management) is managing the process of change, without bringing the enterprise to a standstill. In some products, there is a specification for every item in the structure. If there is a screw, there will be a document with a dimensional drawing of it. The Panasonic capacitor we mentioned earlier will have a detailed drawing, plus the Panasonic manufacturer's information, as well as any other manufacturer that has been deemed able to satisfy the requirement. Since each of these specifications is an internal document, it will (should) be under revision control. If Panasonic changes the part on the spec, then the OEM's spec has changed and needs to be revised. Now that the OEM's spec has changed, this item must be looked at throughout the enterprise for its "where used"—all of the assemblies where this part is present. These assemblies are now subject to having an ECO processed against them—with a full impact analysis. If the top level changes for a family of full box build products, the ECO could have an impact that looks like this:

> *Panasonic has changed their part number...*
>
> *OEM*
> *332-50V001XG is the OEM Spec containing Panasonic, ECO processed to update Spec to Revision "B."*
>
> *A "Where Used" search finds 332-50V001XG to be used on all products, which includes: 10 top-level assemblies; 3 sublevel assemblies; 1 spare parts assembly.*
>
> *An ECO must now be cut to update the bill of material for each assembly, starting with the lowest levels, as the subassemblies' revisions will change and will need to be reflected in the top-level assembly. If the assemblies are marked with the revision, there may be a physical change to the units (i.e., labeling), resulting in added cost.*

This all seems a little absurd: a manufacturer changing the part number of a component resulting in thousands of dollars of administrative costs and a huge resource allocation to keep it all straight. In fact, if the OEM has a contract manufacture for all production, the impact is doubled as the configuration management process is mirrored at the CM.

To limit this type of administrative impact, while ensuring product configuration integrity, various strategies and rules can be implemented.

First, the structure may separate the Parts List and the Final Assembly Drawing. The Final Assembly Drawing has a revision and the reporting marked items do as well. The Parts List/BOM has its own revision and calls out for all of the needed parts, as well as the drawings, declaring their revision and having a value of "0 per" or "ref" (for reference). This enables the OEM to make revisions to component level products and not physically affect the marking of mechanical parts and top-level product revisions. The BOM's identifying part number, however, must be what is ordered from the CM or loaded into the ERP, if subassemblies are to be subcontracted. This will still create administrative work at the OEM and the CM, but will keep rework and physical changes to the products to a minimum.

Another approach is to enter a deviation to a spec, which updates the component record without an ECO. This is typically done in a case like the Panasonic part mentioned above. A "deviation" typically *allows* something different without *requiring* it. For example, if Panasonic changes the part number of the capacitor, then the new number is added to the system, and the old number is still perfectly acceptable. If another manufacturer is approved for the same spec, they can be added via a deviation, as both are now acceptable parts and there is no impact to the current design.

Mechanical deviations can be made to custom parts. If a supplier can get a different grade of raw material faster, then it can be approved with a deviation. One-time deviations can allow for a different component's use or eliminate a potential rejection of a part, if the issue is not impacting to the functionality, but may not be something wanted on a repeat basis.

Deviations do not work when a permanent change is being made to the design. If the Panasonic part was eliminated (for whatever reason) from the AVL on the specification, then a formal ECO would need to be processed and an impact analysis conducted. When/if an ECO is done to a spec, any deviations against it are then cleaned up and formally incorporated.

In any case, deviations and ECOs present a challenge to the enterprise and its business partners. Change management demands strict control, yet the process is far reaching into the organization, both internally and externally, posing a process cycle that bogs down the best of operations.

15. Outsourcing Strategy

Go time! Now that we have covered the industry, what makes the companies in it tick, and what we need to successfully outsource our manufacturing, we can proceed to launch a manufacturing project. The decision has been made: we are going to outsource! And the specifications are clean and detailed for a successful product build at a third party manufacturer.

Objectives

If a start up company is in the initial phases of product development, the objective may be to establish a long term manufacturing partner. Outsourcing for cost reduction may involve balancing supply channels with more than one CM in order to maximize global cost opportunities and maintain a consistent product pipeline. Additionally, a source may be needed for new product introduction. Whatever the quest, the top line objective is to ensure quality product is available for consumption whenever demanded.

As we step through the process of outsourcing, we will focus on new product introduction for electronic assemblies, as this will exercise most of the needs any company will face when outsourcing manufacturing.

Roles and Responsibilities

With every project, in every company, there are specific people that do specific things. We won't rehash the behavioral rants—these roles are easily identified, and are, of course, subject to the human variables good and bad (oops, there we go again!). Assuming all works well, there will be a point person, typically a program manager or a product manager. In a start up, the same individual might wear many hats—the program manager is typically the director of operations as the company starts, then a program manager or materials manager comes on board as the company grows. From the CM's perspective, the lines of communications must be clear, especially in larger organizations. "Who gives the purchase orders?" is a good place to start. Once the decision maker is established, a technical contact for the given project needs to be confirmed (sometimes the same person). On all issues, it is best to keep the primary point of contact involved, or at least appraised of the situation. In government procurement, there is a "POC (Point of Contact)" identified on all requirements.

Scope

Schedule, technical requirements, product content and production volume expand upon the objectives, providing an in-depth look at the expectations of the company with regard to the product's specification and market performance. A documented Scope of Work, or SOW (AKA Statement of Work) is a valuable package for the outsourcing process. In the scope, the requirements for the manufacturing company should be present: capabilities, certifications, etc. The rollout schedule and market expectations will also provide a decent understanding of the capacity required as well as the responsiveness the CM will need to provide.

When searching for a contract manufacturer, a SOW included with the RFP (Request for Proposal) or RFQ (Request for Quotation) documentation enhances the understanding of the requirement, establishes the ground rules for engagement, and adds credibility in a "formalized" fashion to the outsourcing effort.

Example:

Program Overview:

The outsourcing effort will involve two "box level" products involving PCB assembly, cable assembly, final assembly into an enclosure, test, and then pack-out. The products are in development; no working samples exist yet, as the award will consider the supplier's ability to handle new product introduction. The destination market is in pollution monitoring and the production volume will ramp to a few thousand annually, shipping worldwide.

Specific technical requirements:
Surface mount PCB assy – (Ball Grid Array / BGA capable)
In Circuit Test
Mechanical assy
Functional test
Cable assy (can be outsourced to another CM)

Quality requirements:
ISO-certified shop
RoHS – lead free-manufacturing
UL files to be maintained by manufacturer
IPC workmanship

Business requirements:
Turnkey manufacturing
$2-$4 million in awarded business (must be able to buy materials to support)
Potential international version escalating volume to $10+ million, possible offshore manufacturing (TBD)
Virtual factory: all material movement to reside at CM, including direct shipments to end customer, finished goods inventory management, customer returns and repair capability.

Supplier Search

Now that the requirements are known and documented, we turn to the outside world and begin the search. The Internet vastly enhances this process, but we still need a starting point. For an EMS company, the search should begin by matching the size and technology of the "package" to the industry. If the above scope of work were to be $2-$4 million, the top-tier EMS companies would most likely no-bid the requirement. Worse, if they did bid it, they are probably in a temporary situation were they needed to book some business at a given facility, but the fit would be wrong and the long term level of service would most likely be poor, as the EMS provider would satisfy its $50 million customers first. Sizing is important, as the infrastructure of the CM will provide the right level of service if there is a good "fit." If you have the $2-$4 million program and end up in a $100 million CM or division of a CM, you will be 5% of their business. Your POC will probably be a program manager who drew the short straw. They will have other customers to handle, most likely larger ones, so your little program will not be the biggest priority and resources to support you may be limited.

The reverse is also true with respect to fit. If your $4 million program is awarded to a $5 million CM, you are now what is known as "the 600-pound gorilla." You dominate the CM's revenue, as well as their resources. While this may appear to be ideal, the CM may not have the infrastructure you need to successfully manage your program. The business dollars may justify a dedicated program manager, but even if provided, the rest of the organization may not be able to handle the incremental increase in business. Also, the CM will largely feel the impact of your inefficiencies. Another concern is the financial viability of the CM. If your program has a large swing in demand (as in, the wrong way) the inventory pipeline can stop dead in its tracks, crippling the CM's cash flow. By the time your demand returns, it may be too late for the CM.

The above scenario is tempting for all, however. The OEM gets an almost captive manufacturing facility, with top priority on everything. The CM grows the business by a huge chunk, and only has to service one account to get it done. We see this risk being taken daily, because the benefits to the players involved are all too enticing.

Larger OEMs with mature outsourcing infrastructure may have a policy where they address the above. Some will say that they will only represent 20-25% of the CM's revenue. This will give them a definite priority and high level of service at the CM, but their actions alone will not cripple the operation. Some OEMs don't care. EMC Corp. of Massachusetts dominated (and may still) Benchmark Electronics in Hudson, NH, accounting for the majority of their revenue (numbers like this are kept very private, but were rumored to be over 60%). In the late '90s ACT Manufacturing had 60-75% of their revenue come from Chip Com. This customer provided the growth that enabled them to go public, then, as quickly as possible, they brought in other large customers to reduce the risk.

So, a good rule of thumb is to find CMs that can handle your business, both process-wise and financially, but are small enough that you are a significant customer for them.

Location should be in the TCO formula. Some companies go straight offshore to launch the initial product offering, or migrate there as quickly as possible. Others stay local for logistic or technical reasons. It all depends on the market pressure you are under, i.e., what your competition is doing/paying to manufacture their products.

For NPI and initial production, a local, service-oriented CM is best. If the products are destined for offshore manufacturing, then a smaller shop can be used that specializes in prototypes and low-volume production. If production is to stay where it starts, then the above fit is looked for. The SOW should spell this out, even if the transition to a low-cost zone will take years.

Technical needs may warrant a specific search, where only a segment of the market has certain capabilities, such as fiber optic or large environmental testing capabilities. Whatever the needs list bares, there will be suppliers that can support some or all of the requirements. Identifying them up front and culling the ones that cannot do required tasks or processes helps get you to the "short list."

Talk to the right people. In the EMS industry, the component suppliers know the players very well. They know the personality of the companies, the level of in or out of control that they operate under and, of course, if they are paying their bills.

On the initial pass, create a list of candidates. For EMS providers, that list can range from 5-10 companies. The larger number may include offshore options to explore.

RFI / Request for Information

After a brief education on the industry players, the scope of the project is matched to the supply base, resulting in the following list of candidates:

3 suppliers ranging from $10–$50 million, fully capable—all requirements in place
3 Suppliers $5–$20 million, appear to have requirements in place
2 offshore manufacturers
2 sub $10 million, local proto/short run manufacturers

The above should cover all manufacturing needs and allow for several sourcing strategies to be fully evaluated.

The 10 shops are contacted and all available literature/information is requested. The list includes:

Website information
Brochure
Quality manual
Customer references
Supplier references

Banking references

At this point, the candidates' respective salespeople will (should) be all over you. The program overview is supplied in the RFI letter, with notice that a formal SOW may follow, providing there is a "fit" between the two companies. The candidates should respond to the above request and include a description of their capabilities with respect to the requirements.

The RFI phase may eliminate a candidate or two. It is best to have at least two for each scenario: local prototype, production, and offshore. If the list is reduced to one candidate, another should be found. Elimination can occur for almost any reason. Poor credit reports, missing required equipment or technology, or just a bad gut feeling can bounce a candidate.

At this point, site visits are conducted. For local suppliers this is not an expensive proposition. For distant and offshore suppliers, this may be postponed until after the RFP is completed. The site visit is another validation of capability. This is an informal visit that includes a walk through of the factory and some initial conversation about the way they operate and the opportunity the OEM is presenting. The result is a good "sniff" test adding to the gut check.

From the 10 potentials the list may shrink to a hypothetical:

1 supplier ranging from $20–$50 million, fully capable—all requirements in place (with an overseas manufacturing facility)
2 suppliers $5–$20 million, appear to have requirements in place, one with cable assembly in house
1 offshore manufacturer (lower priority)
2 sub $10 million local proto/short run manufacturers

While there is no industry standard on how many suppliers should be bid, a good rule of thumb is three to five. For DOD companies, three bids are required. For an OEM looking for a partner to help them be successful, four or five is not unreasonable. The above short list aligns with a domestic manufacturing strategy that "might" end up offshore in the future. Additionally, this list lends itself to developing a couple of sources: a production facility, plus a prototype/short run supplier.

RFP / Request for Proposal

Assuming all pass the initial RFI phase, we now step forward with the Request for Proposal. For EMS companies this is a significant effort, as the supply chain must be queried to cost all of the components, and the engineering department's participation is needed in the labor and NRE.

The RFP "package" delivered to the CM is the first representation of your company. As detailed earlier, the documentation for the proposal will demonstrate how difficult it will be to "deal with you." A clean, electronic data package and a SOW, if available, will result in a response where the OEM can gauge the CM's ability in the bid phase. The RFP will also define the data you wish to receive in the response, such as costs elements, lead time analysis, and any non-recurring charges.

The quote is often considered the first deliverable by the EMS provider. It does, in fact, provide a looking glass into the enterprise's process control, data management, and technical comprehension (as described in *Core Competence*). Also, how well they respond to the request will demonstrate their ability to work with you.

A response of "No Bid" from a supplier indicates a breakdown in the process. If the RFI phase is done properly, the bidders will respond positively. If the OEM is a start up and funding is providing the operating cash, it should be discussed prior to the bidding. A poor D&B report or other financial issues can cause a 180 degree turnaround at the bid phase. Also, any special business requirements should be addressed in the RFI, such as the holding of finished goods, etc.

The aforementioned package can also impact the quality of the bid response. If the documentation is poor, the engineering group may slow or even stop the bid process out of concerns of being able to meet or interpret the specifications.

During the bid cycle there may be round of questions regarding the specifications or materials. A POC should be established at the outset of the RFP, to facilitate a smooth and timely process.

How quickly these questions are answered will also provide a gauge to the CM's responsiveness.

E-Bid

One of the newer fads is the E-bid, or reverse auction. These are live web events where bidders are given a bid package in advance, run the quotes, then, at a given time, all bid for the award.

Typically these are very large packages involving "lots" of products by commodity. A grouping of similar machined parts totaling a million dollars of estimated revenue can be auctioned off to the lowest bidder on a web event. The bidders are typically cloaked with an ID number and all watch the pricing fall. With moments left, a bidder may take it "into the dirt" and low-ball a number that no one else can touch.

If done right, these reverse auctions can save companies a significant amount of money. The risks are obvious. If a company low-balls to win the business, how can they make money at it? This tactic is known as "taking it off the street," where the business gets awarded and then, the CM has to figure out how to make money off of it. This results in nickel and diming every step of the way, in an attempt to get the program profitable. There is also the risk of the CM re-quoting their "mistake" after it's too late to turn elsewhere. Additionally, the bidders need to be pre-qualified by the company, otherwise risk a new supplier with poor performance and a future mess to clean up in the wake of a nice cost reduction.

Benchmarking

Another type of RFP or bidding worth noting is benchmarking. This is where there is no business awarded, but rather an evaluation of the market's rates and costs is conducted.

Typically the OEM will have conducted some of this during product development, in order to validate the price position in the target market. After development is over and the products are in production, the OEM may launch a benchmarking that looks like an outsourcing award.

This drives CMs and distributors nuts, because it is a waste of time for everyone but the OEM who is just testing the waters, so they can go back to their CM and demand a price reduction.

Evaluation

Now that the bids are in, the decision process starts. First and foremost is price. The cost details, if provided, are compared. For EMS awards, a "costed" bill of materials is reviewed for the best material pricing. "A" item pricing is typically known by the OEM as they have worked with the component manufacturers in the design phase. The different models (if supplied) are compared and analyzed. Certain costs may be challenged, scrutinized, and negotiated. The objective is to get the best of all worlds, but some EMS companies will not give all of the detail, letting their price stand without the analysis.

While pricing settles in, the focus shifts to the rest of the puzzle. The TCA, or Total Cost of Acquisition (AKA TCO, Total Cost of Ownership) must be reviewed. If there is a large distance to travel to the supplier, some sort of allowance/cost must be factored in for that. If the CM is offshore, freight costs and customs must be considered. There are also the undocumented costs of doing business. If an overseas scenario is in play, then there is a lead time to get product overseas via ship. The pipeline is now fixed for a month and any upside opportunity will be missed revenue. For a domestic CM that is far away, there is not only the travel expense, but there may be an increased risk factor in new product introduction that must be weighed.

Other costs include payment terms, warranty of product, etc., which should all be spelled out in the SOW.

Survey
As the lead horse(s) emerges, a site survey is now in order. This may be done with more than one of the finalists. There may even be a pre-survey questionnaire filled out by the supplier. This would provide a general overview of the quality control procedures and systems that are in place—and those that are not.

The team, consisting of a quality engineer, materials representative, and manufacturing/product engineer arrives at the supplier. There may be others, but typically the materials group is in charge of the sourcing effort, and the product engineer is the one who will support the CM technically. And, on this particular day, the quality engineer has total authority over the fate of the CM.

The team typically focuses on two areas: material control and documentation control. Good grades on these core competencies will add greatly to the overall quality control equation. First, there is a review of front end business processes, or the front office. The "I am an order" tour begins. Here, how the customer is handled/serviced is reviewed, and then the customer's manufacturing documentation is routed throughout the facility, until there are work instructions on the floor waiting for the parts to be assembled. The NPI process, including getting MRP actioned in a timely manner can be examined in this exercise. Careful attention to revision control is also key, as well as the ability to control changes to specifications and schedules.

Next, there is the "I am a part" tour. This is where the OEM says, "I am a part and I just hit your dock; take me all the way through the process that puts me in the product and ships it to the customer." The OEM may then back up and ask, "Wait, just how did I get here?" referring to the MRP action to buy and the process through to the receipt at the dock (if they were not covered in the first tour). From there, the part is inspected, accepted or rejected, then moved along to stock, and is issued to a work order and kitted. The entire manufacturing process is walked through, and ultimately, the part is shipped as part of a higher assembly. Throughout this walkthrough, all system transactions, documentation, routings, and procedures are reviewed for consistency and control.

Other areas a survey will examine include the ISO program, if applicable, as well as the procedures and practices on corrective action. The ISO-approved quality system should be up to date with respect to the management review meeting, training, and audits. Corrective action can take place almost anywhere in the organization, but is best reviewed with respect to data interchange with suppliers and customers.

Some surveys involve a scoring system, where there must be a minimum score achieved to do business. There may also be a "conditional approval" where the supplier must make changes in a given period of time to achieve an approved status.

Award

We have sliced and diced the information, and it looks like we have a winner. The pricing has been beaten to death, and then some, and the supplier you like is now the lowest bidder. Also, they have passed muster with the quality survey. They have a reputation with the suppliers for paying their bills and being easy to deal with. Also, they have all of the technical processes in place, so nothing new needs to be learned. Finance has blessed the decision and the product engineer feels comfortable the supplier can meet their needs in manufacturing and service. Everybody internal is on board with the decision.

The winning shop is a $15–$18 million dollar EMS company that is second generation family owned. They are located just thirty minutes away and have a program manager that lives in your town (since it is a hypothetical, why not make it perfect!). While they outsource the cable assemblies, they remain competitive with the vertically integrated shops. They do not have much of a finished goods warehouse, but the President/owner made you comfortable with his plan to create dedicated space for your finished goods and repairs.

If only it happened this way in real life. But, you can come close with due diligence.

The contract is negotiated. Remember, "They're more like guidelines..." The CM is looking for the OEM to sign up to inventory liabilities, and the OEM is looking for the CM to sign up to scheduling rules and quality standards. Payment terms and whose truck is used round things out. This is not to say the contract is a quick or easy thing. Au contraire!

Every word and sentence needs to be analyzed for its potential impact. Larger companies will have a legal resource for this. Even in the standard looking stuff there may large risks or points to be negotiated. With a *change of venue* clause, for example, should litigation occur, one party could move the proceedings a thousand miles away to another branch office, in an attempt to increase the time and expenses of the other party (seen it). Product warranty should only be for the workmanship of the product, not what happens out in the field. If something catastrophic does happen, the lawsuits will fly regardless, but establish the guidelines for day-to-day business.

The scheduling and cost models are front burner issues and there may be a schedule of products that gets amended from time to time, but it's best to agree to a model that does not require such maintenance. And the model should be reviewed over and over.

Believe it or not!

One of the largest, world-class OEMs on the planet outsourced the manufacturing of one of its smaller product lines. This allowed them to close a factory that was not running efficiently. The award was in the $12–$15 million range. Equipment was sold to the EMS provider, and there were some staffing transfers to facilitate the transition.

The product line was a mix of small box builds that shared a common set of PCBs and, depending on model and destination (country), the top level would be configured as they were ordered.

The contract was negotiated, establishing a cost model that allowed reasonable rates and profit margins, yet yielded a cost savings to the OEM. At the point of the first kit drops, the costs for the initial build releases were rolled up and supplied to the OEM.

"NO WAY!" the OEM shouted when they saw the price.

The model was reviewed and everything was dead on at the PCB level. The box level was the problem. The OEM added the top-level material costs to the much analyzed PCBs, and the purchase price was now in line with their analysis. So why was the CM's price so high?

The EMS company then politely advised that the agreed to profit needed to be added to the top-level material, which blew the model used to award the business!

It was far too late to negotiate.

The nod also goes to one of the prototype shops. At $2–$3 million dollars, they were deemed a fit, but too small to handle full production or any upside to the program (even though they said, "Bring it on!"). They receive a different, small project to open up the relationship. This establishes the "Plan B" insurance policy on getting to market.

In our perfect hypothetical world, the prototype shop would also make cable assemblies, allowing for full capability in a shop just five minutes away. Production cable assemblies could be sourced, or, at a minimum quoted by this shop as well, keeping the primary CM fully aware of the smaller shop's presence—and hunger!

The overseas scenario can be addressed down the road, if necessary. The business cycle just completed provided information and education that can be of value if and when the time comes.

The primary award is now announced and manufacturing agreements are executed with the new suppliers. The cost model is reviewed and defined, one more time, so there will be no need for negotiation—in the short term at least. If there was a conditional quality approval, there will be a corrective action plan drafted to remedy any issue the survey kicked up.

16. Production Ramp

Remember, this is a transaction-based business. Nothing happens without a purchase order. Sure, the engineers can bond and discuss special fixtures and maybe even do a little DFM review, but the long pole in the tent is materials, and they are not going to budge without an MRP roll, which takes a customer order to trigger it. The small prototype shop stands at the ready.

Assuming the contract negotiation does not drag on and impact the schedule, the initial orders are placed. This is a critical point in the relationship, as the requirements are low, and the commitments and costs are high.

Alpha
The very first builds are for proof of concept and design. This involves build quantities of just a couple of units. The EMS provider has the largest expense for the smallest revenue. When it comes to new product introduction the expression is, "You can't charge enough!"

The reason for this is the investment the CM makes. They go through the same exact steps as a 100 or 1000 unit run, for five to ten units. The BOM must be structured, and MRP must be driven to action each component, as well as the establishing of a stocking location for all new items. The overhead expense to get this done, and to set up and support the short run production makes this a loser in most production houses. Some OEMs will build the alpha units in house, or at their design house, if engaged with one.

The smaller prototype shop is the answer (even though the larger EMS company touted a core competence of new product introduction). They can make money on these jobs, because they do not have the big infrastructure related processes to contend with and can run with a lower overhead cost making the shorter runs profitable.

One of the desires for the engineering team, however, is to run new products down the line where they will see their full production volumes being built. This is true DFM and a proper NPI practice. The value of this is somewhat vague. Yes, it makes sense, but the volume shop may run the prototypes down a separate line anyway, so as not to interfere with revenue. And the smaller shop can handle a mix of turnkey and consigned parts, because difficult parts are often bought in small volumes by the engineers and are on hand to support the alpha builds.

So, depending on the responsiveness and flexibility of your CM, as well as the cost structure, there may be a place where the second, close to home, quick turn shop makes sense (remember the example of Cooper Perkins pulling the job from a CM) for those critical first 1–5 units (and their subsequent modifications).

Beta

Beta and pilot are sometimes synonymous. Beta usually refers to a smaller run of 5–25 for extended testing and perhaps a few marketing samples to be demonstrated to customers. There is usually at least one more *spin* of the board after the beta build (a "spin" is when the bare board-PCB is changed.) This is a major ECO and a major milestone in product development, as production tooling and test fixtures are held back until the PCB layout is deemed production ready). Here, the EMS company should be fully engaged with the design team, as the guts of the product are more stable and the DFM mindset is engaged on the next set of revisions. Materials should be involved as well, and the major technology components can be worked for sourcing as the cost roll up (quotation) is established by the EMS company (with a close eye on them by the OEM).

Pilot

This is often the first production run. Some of the units may be already sold or promised to end customers. The volumes are typically 50+, depending on the complexity. A smaller, consumer product may run hundreds to create marketing samples, etc. Whatever the volume, the purpose of the plot run is to do a final sanity check on the manufacturing process and product validation (test), without committing too much inventory ($) to finished goods, just in case. In fact, the projected build plan may be "on order" at the time of a pilot run, with volatile components being held back.

During alpha, beta, and pilot runs, there will be close interaction between both parties' engineering disciplines. This requires some "letting go" from a program management standpoint, as the activity level and the schedule warrant it. The basic rule is, when money is discussed, as in tooling, fixtures, etc., the team needs to know.

Managing the program during this phase can be challenging, as there is a high level of activity, communication, and expense that needs to be managed, monitored, and accounted for. In larger EMS companies, there will be NPI teams and meetings focused on tracking and scheduling NPI into the factory.

> In the late 1990s, ACT Manufacturing was growing and had passed the $100 million mark. Running seven surface mount lines, ACT averaged one new product into production every business day.

If not managed carefully, NPI projects will collide with one another, as well as disrupt the month's revenue stream.

Production
At last!

For some, this is where things get exciting. For others, double yawn. It is those true "ops" people who thrive on balance, stability, reaction time, and repeatable efficiency, that make a factory tick. The daily grind involves running the gambit on all fronts. Daily material shortage meetings, reschedules, downtime, quality yields, and of course, the monthly revenue objectives all keep things lively in the world of operations management.

Production orders must be carefully maintained on the CM's books to keep the materials pipeline full, or risk missing market opportunity. The OEM would like the least amount of order coverage, as it presents liability. The CM would like the most amount of order coverage, as it presents backlog! The lead time of the assembly plays into the required order coverage and helps create an ordering strategy. If there is one part that has an abnormally long lead time, then a purchase order for that part alone may be placed, to channel a year's worth and only create liability for one component. The top-level product can now be scheduled tighter.

If the intent were to transfer production to a low-cost region/volume facility as the volumes ramped up, this would have been stated in the SOW in the original bid. If so, there is now another sourcing business cycle and NPI phase to start the transition to the new supplier. A cut off might involve an overlap to ensure product availability. Some products, like consumer electronics go straight into production offshore, as the CM is vertically integrated and production tooling is all done just once, overseas. The local CM's role, if any, is to support development work and prototype building.

APC of Rhode Island developed a new product requiring an outer housing. This housing was initially metal, but was to be made of plastic, in India, for production. The sheet metal house bid $20 for the first thousand units to get the product launched, then the plastic part, sub $3, would be cut in as India came on line. The product was *released to market, and the factory in India was not ready. The sheet metal house "quick turned" over 17,000 units in three months!*

17. Sustaining / SCE

For the OEM, the ongoing managing of the EMS partner falls under Supply Chain Execution. Many books and practices exist detailing the how's and why's of managing and optimizing the supply chain. From lean to JIT, it's all about having the right amount of stuff at the right time—and no liability for more. Of course, the stuff is also at the lowest possible price, but that fun abuse session is now over.

The SCE professional is tightly connected to the product and demand managers at the OEM, and the program manager (and for large programs, the materials group) at the CM. They create and manage the conduit between the enterprises, formalizing all communications and commitments. As mentioned earlier, not only is this where the purchase orders come from, but also some of the bigger decisions on *who does what to whom* originate here.

Order Commitments

Order coverage at the CM, as mentioned above, aligns materials, as well as scheduling capacity.

EDI interchanges and pull systems can be done, but for the most part, contract manufacturing, in all market segments, remains a reactive business where a purchase order is the only catalyst to production. To that end, the manufacturing agreement must outline the rules. Often, the rules are kept simple. The OEM places orders and the CM buys parts—but just enough parts to cover the orders. Any minimum purchase requirements must be approved in advance. Rather than manage an approval process for this, the CM may provide an Excess Inventory List as part of the quotation. Or, general statements in the contract will set policy toward material commitments.

A **rolling forecast** is one where a product can be scheduled out for, say, a year, with the first three months being a firm commitment, or "hard order," and the other 9 months having no commitment but useful for general information. This at least provides the CM with the lifecycle knowledge of the products, allowing them size up capacity for months ahead. Each month, another month is locked in and the schedule is adjusted, with rules on the second and third months' flexibility.

Beyond this, there is not much sophistication in the managing of supply chain orders. This is not to say that there cannot be. But, let's remember how this whole industry is set up: it's a very lean and traditional operational methodology. If an OEM wants to be state of the art in business practice, they had better be prepared to lead by example, and work with the CM, as they are limited by design to succeed in a change in their business practices.

And let's not believe that the OEM is all knowing and the teacher in best practices.

> The mighty Motorola itself with Six Sigma, Motorola University, EDI order exchange, etc., divested a manufacturing facility to a local, large EMS provider. The business was about $7 million per year in a high mix of low to moderate volume.
>
> The CM heard it all: they had lot sizes of one, three-day manufacturing cycle times, SPC, and a team of just about every type of expert. And everything was built to order. The CM needed to step up.
>
> Then, a bill came for hundreds of thousands of dollars to transfer ownership of the balance of WIP. But there were no orders for the assemblies, which were in various stages of completion throughout the factory.
>
> "These were the 'Kan Ban Squares!' and they needed to be transferred," insisted Motorola. Now the three-day cycle times and miniscule lot sizes started to make sense.

"No thanks," replied the CM. *"We will buy that stuff when there are hard orders for it."*

Cost Reductions

Moving the business to a low-cost region or a re-award via an E-bid are indeed ways to cut costs (a TCO formula should be in place when evaluating any type of cost-cutting program with the supply base), but there are also periodic cost reductions that can be worked with the existing manufacturing partner.

There are several ways to achieve cost reductions. Earlier, we mentioned the brutal way in which SCI was tormented each quarter by Racal. Is it safe to say that they would not have achieved the price points if they weren't so tenacious? Yes. But, look at the total costs, including the lost revenues, which also occurred due to poor execution of the team and the resultant lack of desire of the CM to service them (business at a loss). Then add the costs associated with moving their manufacturing to a new supplier. One could even speculate on their own contribution to their evaporation from the market.

There is no question that a program to reduce costs must be in place with any outsourcing effort. Besides, it's in the blood of the materials team to go out and get a better deal. Some of the better cost reduction achievements are measured on more than just PPV. Let's go back to the contract. Typically, in a significant outsourcing effort, like the one we simulate in this study, there is a contract that covers orders, scheduling and rescheduling rights, and defines the cost models. It may also set the rules on a cost pass through—when a component's cost changes and the purchase order is amended to reflect the new price roll up.

Often, with market or CM related cost reductions, the CM will get to burn the existing (higher priced) inventory, and benefit from the savings for a few months, then pass it on to the OEM. If the OEM negotiates a better price or specs in a cheaper part, they will get the savings when it is realized.

When both parties are in agreement, there can be great successes in cost reduction without impacting either company's bottom line. If an OEM is to go down this road, the expectation should be spelled out in the SOW from the outset of the search for the proper supplier.

Cost reductions can also be achieved in lowering defect rates and making improvements in the manufacturing process. These are some of the smaller gains, but sometimes the sweetest, as the passion for manufacturing efficient product rises to the top. The larger (remember the 70/30 rule) gains result from beating down the supply chain for material price reductions.

QBR

The **quarterly business review** is a forum where the executives and team members present data regarding the relationship—and the players in the relationship reveal their true feelings. There will be a tone or atmosphere to the room, where you will know if the relationship is working or not. The statistics will support the health of the relationship.

When times are good, these are great meetings. When things are bad, they can be grueling and argumentative. It's the teams' working through the daily issues, the schedules, and the firefighting that made the quarter and year end happen for both. A good QBR should be the celebration of hard work.

1990s Telecom Heyday:
The defect was one found before any product shipped to the end customer(s). While the boards passed test, it was discovered that the circuit board's barrel-shaped holes, or vias, were incomplete with regard to the copper plating, leading one to suspect there may

be internal issues in the circuitry (which the vias were part of). The OEM's and CM's teams assembled.

The circuit boards were not to spec. Not acceptable to either team's quality standards, nor IPC standards. All agreed. The bare boards were worth hundreds dollars each—and there were hundreds of them. No question the manufacturer would be liable. But the first problem was that they were already assembled (read: soldered) by the EMS provider. There were thousands of dollars of parts on each board (which would be scrap). This represented hundreds of thousands of dollars of cost for the CM, not to mention the lost revenue.

The second problem was that the boards went into systems the OEM needed to sell, representing millions of dollars in revenue; their factory stood poised to receive the product.

The third problem was that it was late December and both companies were at their year end. And, yes, both companies were public.

There was no need to escalate the problem to upper management at either company. Besides, what does IPC really know about quality! The verdict was easy: if the boards passed test, they were fine.

The year end went off well for both companies and the subsequent QBR never mentioned the crisis. Chalk up one for true partnerships!

Disengagement

When an outsourcing effort fails, revenues are placed in jeopardy and a new source must be brought in quickly. If a global strategy is in place, the source may be the existing contract manufacturer, if they have a global footprint and the transition did not work.

In a low-cost region failure, the OEM may face the fact that costs are going back up. The OEM has reset their internal cost models and adjusted their standards to the new, lower cost of acquisition. COGS is down, profits are up. To undo this, there is pain—much pain.

After the bloodshed in the meeting which asked: "How the #@$! did we get into this situation?" there must be a plan to get manufacturing back on track with the least amount of financial impact. As mentioned earlier, for North America, enter Mexico. A discussion with the VP of business development at a top 10 EMS reveals that their Mexico facilities are enjoying a surge of new business migrating (back) from the Far East. Those OEMs that chose to go offshore and failed were now looking at a return, and Mexico's lower labor rates could soften the blow of the transition.

One scenario is to balance two sources of supply—one domestic and one offshore. The larger EMS companies have the facilities to do this. But even at a smaller level this strategy can work, provided the shops selected are the right business fit. If your company has a moderate volume and mix of products, they can be separated into the right manufacturing companies. The previous story of the failed program with the controls company may have fared better if they had a very small CM in Mexico in the mix.

In the event of a **cancellation** the CM is expected to return for credit all materials that can be sold back to the distributors and manufacturers. Any non-cancelable / non-returnable items would be identified and signed off in the same manner as above. This will all work fine until the numbers get big or the cancellation is disengagement, rather than the discontinuing of a product.

When that happens, the wagons are circled and the lawyers are called. This is not theory. As anyone can imagine, regardless of what is right or wrong (morally and legally), the bottom line is the bottom line. Remember, compensation dictates behavior, and when the individuals involved in the problem see their compensation is in jeopardy…

For the CM, remember the business methodology: customer places order, CM buys parts. Anything beyond that is now on the table as risk. If the program manager was preparing for the lawsuit all along, this will be much less painful. Furthermore, if the account management was in line with this study's definition of the role, there would have been quarterly business reviews, proper execution of change management, resolution of excess inventory as it occurred, and a current receivables position. The risk would be only to the current point in time, the products in WIP, the excess inventory required to execute the build plan, etc. The reconciliation of the inevitable will go much more smoothly and without some of the emotion that typically goes along with a break up.

The CM's customers will come and go. Sometimes the CM screws up and there is no recovery. Sometimes the OEM is acquired, sometimes they outgrow their CM, and sometimes they go out of business. And sometimes their name is Racal…

18. Summation

A contract manufacturer cannot create the next great thing and stir demand to increase revenues; they must seize the opportunities as they arise, while, at the same time, limit idle resources- the ones required to support any upside. The ability to do this while controlling processes, inventory, and efficiently building quality products defines the bottom line. Balancing this is the daily business of a CM.

The skill sets and models may vary, but the formula is the same. Asset turn momentum is the core competence that keeps all contract manufacturers alive, whether they are a sheet metal fabricator, plastics molder, or EMS provider. Idle time is an open wound on the balance sheet and can take down a healthy CM in short order. In the same light, inventory, while considered an asset (financially), has toppled billion dollar EMS companies in just a few months, as there is an enormous, often financed cash flow that must be maintained.

While the job shops may not be as sensitive to demand shifts due to their materials/value add model, their fate lies on capital equipment and work force utilization. The crushing blows may not come as quickly as sitting on a mountain of excess inventory, but when large economic shifts come, as they did in 1998 and 2001, the results can be devastating if an enterprise is leveraged from financed equipment or expansion.

The EMS industry has reinvented itself in the last twenty years, resultant from the explosion of the consumer electronics industry. From its roots in the '60s, we saw the "build to print" carpenter/architect profitably doing for less what an OEM would spend on an internal effort. We then saw the "carpenter" advanced to the virtual factory, selling a "core competence" model of manufacturing vs. technology and marketing. Finally, we have the ODM model, or EMS provider with full design services. Here the CM holds virtually the same skill sets as the OEM, and is often vertically integrated and globally positioned. Having the means, we now see some EMS/ODM companies morphing into OEMs, cutting out the "middle man" and realizing full OEM profit by marketing their own brands of products.

At the OEM, in addition to sourcing in the lowest cost regions where possible, the latest lean initiatives have pushed as much liability as possible back onto the CM, testing its delicate asset turn model. This can devastate the cash flow and result in the low margin cost model eating the EMS provider alive. The case has been made that Solectron was further weakened by Cisco's "lean" initiative, where massive amounts of inventory liability where pushed downstream to the supply chain. Companies do this while referring to their victims as their *"value chain"* (isn't that cute?).

Inside all of these enterprises, we see people (the root of all evil). Agendas, bonuses, and internal conflicts compound the variable of individual ability. The results are that world-class manufacturers are sometimes not so world-class. Add the enterprise's need for financial performance, especially at the close of the quarter or year, and behavior and practices can violate all logic and many laws.

The future of contract manufacturing is uncertain. The migration of manufacturing to low-cost regions has resulted in a surplus of domestic CM capacity, which keeps competition fierce and margins low. On a global level, the EMS/ODM providers show in-the-dirt margins, net profits of less than 5%, and often subzero profit lines during any type of economic recovery, as survival means keeping the pig fed.

We now operate in a brutal environment where the OEMs look for the company that can produce the products that will pass inspection for the lowest cost. This results in the sourcing of manufacturing in places that have the lowest labor rates, sometimes less than humane treatment to its work force, and the least amount of regulations on how the enterprise operates in its community or affects its environment.

This not so altruistic behavior is driven by the civilized world's demand for cheap gadgets and gizmos, and the quest for strong earnings per share by the companies that supply these goods.

Now in 2009, we are faced with a global economic crisis unlike anything the planet has ever seen. The economic interdependence of many nations has the world sitting on edge, waiting for a bright sign.

Will the contract manufacturing industry survive? Does it need saving?

As in 2002, we will see a shake out. The last one thinned the herd, leaving a stronger breed throughout the value chain that was conscious of commitments and less trusting of their business partners. But many did not heal, especially the big dogs. The gaping hole left in domestic, higher cost manufacturing, walked on as a wounded animal. As we started the second decade, the new order of electronics manufacturing had not only matured, but low-cost manufacturing regions—China—had come up the curve and was now competing for the higher tech manufacturing that had previously not been trusted in such a region. The survivors of the telecom implosion looked East for lower costs to maximize profits as they struggled for market share.

The industry spotlight, however, quickly swung over to the new handheld gadgets we listened to and talked into. The iPod was out and the cost of laptops was falling. PDAs were the rage, not to mention the dramatic increase in electronics in our automobiles, right down to GPS navigation screens. Again, eyes looked to the east to make these gadgets at affordable prices.

While the domestic EMS companies fought for the table scraps, the largest firms started increasing manufacturing capacity in China and Malaysia, and developing new capacity in such places as India, Eastern Europe, and Vietnam. The current economic crisis has ceased much of this expansion and caused a rapid scaling back in an attempt to match capacity to the reduced demand.

The herd is back in the crosshairs and the weak are about to give their all to make the breed even stronger—and then some.

Life will go on. There will be casualties. But there will also be people with a little money who will not be able to resist the next gizmo that holds their songs, sends messages to their friends, or makes their coffee while they are in the shower. The manufacturing industry will survive and adjust to the economy as it sorts itself out.

What will the new order look like? When the dust settles, will it be business as usual?

As chanted throughout this study, the asset turn model is the powder keg in contract manufacturing. Turning over the large, floating block of money tied up in materials determines the financial performance of the CM. If a CM turns $1 million in revenue annually and 70% of that is material cost, then $700K has to be laid out for materials. Remember, on the $1 million, there will be a net profit of less then $100K. But, if you can turn over your inventory seven times per year, you would then only need $100K of cash to manage the materials portion of the business. At 10%, profit, you would achieve a $70K income on a $100K investment (materials only, the factory expense would obviously need to be profitable as well). This is what drives the turnkey EMS industry.

Look at Flextronics: $30 billion a year in revenue, 2%–3% profit. If materials account for 70%, that's $21 billion in material purchases. But if turns were seven, that's $3 billion in cash to manage the materials piece of the business, which generates $0.63 Billion in profits (on 21 billion in material spend.) That's a 21% return. Not bad. Asset utilization comes into play on the remaining $9 billion of value add revenue.

Now increase the turns by one and get another percent profit. Or get a little PPV and send that to the bottom line. This floating block of money is often financed, as it is a variable need. And, as you would expect, the financing is not free, thus, another eroding force on quoted thin margins. Add value to this block of borrowed money and then have the customers say slow down or stop, and you have the train wreck—instantly!

The largest companies' obsession with growth and market share, along with the feeding frenzy like-behavior of the lower tiers, due to a surplus of capacity, has all but abandoned best business practices from a financial sense and created a "buy the business" mentality.

One possible solution to the dilemma is to bring back the consignment model. Unfortunately, this will never happen, as the OEMs enjoy not having their capital tied up to support their shot in the dark forecasts. Nor will the EMS companies be able to concede that the elimination of the majority of their revenue is a good thing.

But for the moment, let's entertain the thought. First, the world is much different than it was ten years ago. Any EMS provider of size will have strategic relationships with the major distributors of components, even an in-house stores program.

Managing cash flow through these economic swings has become an art form, and the sophistication of transferring money can allow for some very creative strategies. Raytheon, for example employed the use of credit cards for materials purchases. Terms of payment also stimulate cash flow with discounts for early remittance.

Combine the above with the OEM's thirst for cost reduction and the door cracks open for a new strategy.

If an in-house stocking program exists with Arrow Electronics and Avnet Electronics (the two largest distributors in the world), the opportunity to have the majority of materials supplied by them presents itself. We have seen both players in the same stock room at CMs with less than $50 million in revenue, so this concept isn't restricted to the top ten.

Optimally, the part numbering strategy by the CM would be one that uses the customer's part number. To Pareto the bill of material of an assembly, the cost drivers will be less than 20% of the line items. These can be supplied, as required, by the two distributors, but the billing goes to the end customer. A few other strategic components, such as the PCB will need to be handled separately, but this has been done successfully in the past. If not all of the "A" and "B" items, then perhaps the top ten, or a strategic chip set can be put into a program.

Although we said it made sense to take the iPod offshore, let's revisit our assumptions one more time:

80 GB version:
$ 110.00   Hard drive
$ 9.00   LCD screen
$ 8.50   Broadcom chip
$ 6.00   Lion battery
$ 5.80   SoC
$ 3.00   Wolfson Codec
$ 2.50   Click wheel
$ 9.00   Aluminum case

$153.80 total "A" item content. (Balance of material: $27.20)
$181.00 total material cost estimate on tear down.

Source: Katie Marsal, Apple Insider

If a CM were to allow a 10% markup, the adder on the "A" items would be $15.38. Assuming it costs the OEM 2% to manage the supply chain on theses items—about $3.08, a $12.30 cost reduction would be achieved in the partial consignment model. In the lower cost regions of the US this could offset the labor difference in going to the other side of the planet to manufacture.

This would, however, bring the OEM to the party. No longer can the OEM behave like the 600-pound gorilla, bashing about, and getting whatever it wants at just about any cost. The OEM must now feel the pain of their poor planning and unreasonable demands. All of the adverse affects of slow inventory turns, excess liability, and the added expense of operating inside of normal lead times will now be shared by the OEM. But the three way relationship and sharing of data with the distributors will make everyone's asset turns skyrocket.

This concept, while financially sound for the industry, may be doomed from the start. It's completely adverse to the latest lean initiatives to have the OEM participate in additional risk and execution when both could be taken on by the supply chain. Also, why would an OEM want to have any skin in the game and feel the effects of their actions on their cash flow when they don't have to?

But let's look at the cost of your CM filing Chapter 11 after piping all of your material, building to forecast, and then having the pipe shut down for 3 months on an RoHS violation (committed by the OEM.) Operating on a 3% profit puts any enterprise at risk—quickly.

As long as the feeding frenzy continues, the lowest margins in a total turnkey scenario will live on. But when the OEM needs a manufacturing service that will satisfy a certain business need, they will pay a more for it, providing those in charge do not have other motivations. Only an OEM can drive this new model. But what if the cost was negligible? The additional "cost" will be of an internal nature—to manage consigned "A" items. The materials manager at the OEM has (should have) a core competence to successfully source and manage parts, no? Outsourcing a $10 million program to the shop that best fills their needs, at a single digit percentage of markup, is the goal. So, getting there can be done the old way of negotiating, possibly ending up at the wrong shop based on a price need, or by crafting a program that allows the CM to make an above current market margin, while the OEM has a TCO lower than targeted.

It must first make financial sense to the OEM. Their supply chain expert must create, validate, and convince the enterprise that a model such as this is a good idea. Lean initiatives promote the virtual factory, with one line item on order for assembly and one invoice to be paid as those assemblies are received. This is a very compelling argument for a turnkey strategy. But what if the same cost savings of going to Asia could be realized with a new materials strategy?

If 60%–80% of the materials is supplied by the OEM, and the OEM's cost to manage that is negligible, then the labor savings by going offshore has been offset by the savings of the CM's profit margin on the materials.

Simple model:

A circuit board assembly has $100 PO (sell) price.

$70 Material cost
$14 Material markup (20%)
$16 Labor and O/H (with profit)

Or,

$60 Materials consigned by the OEM
$10 Turnkey materials
$3 Material markup (30%)
$16 Labor, O/H (with profit)

$89 sell price

All things being equal, there is an 11% reduction in cost.

To go offshore, the $16 labor and overhead could be reduced by the same amount, or even a little more. The true cost of acquisition, lead time, and market logistics (revenue risks) would then be compared with the cost to manage the "A" items.

If labor and overhead came in at $2 on the overseas bid, the total would be $86 versus the $89.

At 10,000 units per year, the analysis would be as follows:

$1,000,000 in spend. Cost savings on "A" item consignment program = $110,000, vs. additional $30K in savings to go offshore ($86 vs $89), yields a 1.5 % increase in profits on revenue, 3% cost savings on COGS.

Cost of Acquisition for offshore production = "Y"
Cost of local "A" item management / $600,000 annual spend = "Z"

One of the enablers of this concept is the distributors' ever increasing willingness to manage in-house stores at the larger CMs where there is enough projected business to staff a person to administer a small stockroom of components. The majority of the 70% identified above can (typically) be placed in the program, with the OEM being the financial point of contact. As the material is pulled by the CM, the invoicing of the "A" items goes to the OEM. The OEM negotiates their own terms with the distributor, and the receivables are created only when inventory is used to create products by the CM.

The difference (additional cost) to the OEM are more administrative than cash flow oriented as the invoice for the final assembly outsourced will be split between CM and distributor, and should be only days apart.

Once the program is up and running, other items, such as custom enclosures, or a unique connector that cannot through the distribution stores program can be handled on an individual basis, being evaluated for the turnkey or consignment program—possibly creating another supplier to manage for the OEM, if warranted. With "best practices" eyes shifting over to the Accounting Department, sophisticated order management and payment practices are looked at in the Cost of Acquisition model, versus overseas freight, travel, and logistics expenses.

If the volumes were 10x at one million units, the additional savings to go offshore would be $300K warranting more a detailed costs analysis.

The downside to the CM is one of revenue. EMS providers are top line (total revenue) oriented, hence today's market conditions. The $10 million outsourcing program, if run this way, is now only a $3 million package to the CM. Revenues are lowered, and the sales weasel who had just leased a new BMW is now crying after recalculating his commission. And the CEO wants to know why revenue is considerably below the projected "number."

The reality, however, is that profits are up, risk is down, and the customer is not going to beat the tar out of you on cost every quarter. The relationship can focus on the mission, and not look forward to Racal's QBR as profiled earlier.

In fact, if Racal had followed this model, the 15% needed to stabilize the program would have been recognized earlier, quoted properly, and the tenacious materials group would have saved more in the elimination of the markup on the "A" items. Alas, this would have failed too, as the program's "value" to SCI probably would not have been worth the effort.

Another concern is the control the OEM gains by supplying a piece of the puzzle that can halt manufacturing. This leverage is not something the CM wants the customer to have and the terms of how this is handled should be spelled out in advance.

This model is not a hypothetical. It has been proven at large and small CMs:

A program awarded to Wire Techniques, in Chelmsford, Mass, has $225 of material content per assembly. The top eight or nine items represented $190.00 of material cost.

For the initial build of 500, the "A" items were consigned. The $35 dollars of the "C" class material had a 30% margin on it. The labor to create the final assembly was significant: over $150.

The customer now wanted to convert the "A" items over to turnkey. The 30% markup would not fly. The forecast was for 1000–1500 units. That's $190K of "A" item purchase.

At a 10% markup, the CM would not accept the deal, because there was too much cost and risk. For a 20% markup, the customer would be spending an additional $38K in 12 months to outsource the management of eight items—also unacceptable.

The final outcome is a $250 sell price, with the customer supplying eight items for each build. The cost to the customer to manage the items is considered small, as they have a person on staff who can spend a few hours for each release—the total annual cost being nowhere near the 10% markup of $19K, not to mention the $38K at 20%. Additionally, the cash flow to support this was $19K per 100 units (the average build quantity.)

The CM has a program of half the revenue as projected, but there is less cash required by the CM to execute, less risk on a catastrophic downside, and the customer's cost objectives are met, while bringing a gross margin of 30% to the program.

In this model there is no "in-house store" or sophisticated ordering or planning. The small customer needs the local facility to develop and refine functional test of the units, as well as the prototype capability to model new products based on the design. The customer literally "swings by" for coffee and drops off the consigned parts as required.

The trend here is to turn the EMS model into the job shop model, where the Value Add far exceeds the material content.

On a larger scale, the distributors would locate their stores at the CM, but their customer will be the OEM. The relationship shifts back to the OEM even thought the CM is manufacturing the products. Real best practices, value chain, and all those trendy buzzwords would actually come into play. But, this will only happen when everyone has a stake in the game.

So how are you doing?
We haven't forgotten you, the kid who was suddenly and unwillingly thrown into this unforgiving industry. Hopefully, you have learned a lot about how the contract manufacturing industry has evolved and how it operates on a day to day basis.

While you are a smaller player, the world's economy and globalization of manufacturing has reached out and touched you, trashing your bottom line. Yet there is hope. You, unlike many others, have business. In fact, your revenue line is climbing. All of your pay rates and bid rates are in line with the industry, and the data says handsome profits are right around the corner. Hopefully, wherever there is a loss or inefficiency, you can now address it—for the long term. Un-fun, harsh decisions may have to be made about staffing, and even the worst case scenario of closing a facility must be considered.

It is time to take a deep breath, and go back to the first chapter. It's all on the table for you to be a successful contract manufacturer!

TLA / Three Letter Acronyms

The manufacturing industry is riddled with initials and buzzwords. Below is a quick glossary of these acronyms, abbreviations, and slang expressions heard daily in the industry.

Actual – a historical point of data (time or financial) typically compared with a standard data point.

    Alpha – *In product development, the first unit produced. See beta, proto, pilot, DFM.*

    AML – *Approved Manufacturers List – A listing of manufacturers that can provide a specified part or product, typically to be made into a higher assembly. Synonym: AVL, QPL.*

    APICS – *American Production and Inventory Control Society. A manufacturing industry association.*

    AVL—*Approved Vendor List. A listing of manufacturers that can provide a specified part or product, typically to be made into a higher assembly. Synonyms: AML, QPL.*

    Beta—1. *In product development, the second build, or a small quantity of units to prove out a concept. See alpha, proto, pilot, DFM.*
2. *In software, a user or site where an application is used for proving and developing a final production version.*

    BOM—*Bill of Material – The document listing all of the materials/parts to manufacture a higher assembly. See CM, PLM, AVL.*

    CAD – *Computer Aided Design.*

    CAM—*Computer Aided Manufacturing.*

CFM—*Customer Furnished Material. Where an OEM supplies the raw materials to the CM. See turnkey.*

Channel—*1. Supplier, typically a distributor of electronic components.*
2. To award or pipeline products to a supplier.

CM—*1. Contract Manufacturer. Manufacturing service provider.*
2. Configuration Management. Engineering function or software, which controls and maintains product design documentation. See BOM, AVL, PLM.

CSA – *Canadian Standards Association. Like UL (Underwriter's Laboratory) an agency that certifies material and products for safety.*

DMR—*Discrepant Material Report – A document to tag and manage non-conforming material.*

COD – *Cash on Delivery. A credit status where one must pay for goods when they are received.*

COGS—*Cost of Goods Sold. A summation of the standard costs to manufacture items shipped in a given time period.*

DFM -*Design for Manufacture. The practice of considering the existing industry wide equipment and technologies when designing a product, so that it can be manufactured efficiently.*

DFT -*Design for Test. The practice of considering the test and validation requirements of a product in the design phase, so that it can be validated more efficiently when in production.*

DL – *Direct Labor. A status of an employee or financial data point that is directly related to making products (see O/H.)*

DOD—*Department of Defense.*

DTS—*Dock to Stock. Supplier management program that eliminates incoming inspection.*

DWG – *Drawing. Sometimes a file extension for a specification, .dwg*

E-Bid – *An on line, reverse auction to award a purchase order to the lowest bidder. Typically a timed event with all bidders present, lowering their prices until time expires—or a bidder is so low, no one will offer lower.*

EMS—*Electronic Manufacturing Service – Contract manufacturing company supporting the electronics industry. See CM.*

ERP—*Enterprise Resource Planning . A system or software application that manages material, scheduling, inventory, and finance in manufacturing companies. See MRP.*

ESS—*Environmental Stress Screening. A test process where the products are cycled through large temperature swings and/or vibrated to induce shock.*

FCT -*Functional Test. A validation process where the product is tested while performing its designed functions.*

FOB—*Freight On Board / Free on Board – Point of ownership for product shipment.*

HALT *Highly Accelerated Life Testing. A type of ESS that attempts to identify failures over a (simulated) long period of time.*

HASS *Highly Accelerated Stress Screening. A type of ESS that attempts to identify failures from intense operations or harsh environments.*

HVAC—*Heating, Ventilation, and Air Conditioning.*

ICT—*In Circuit Test – A test for printed circuit board assemblies involving a "bed of nails" fixture to validate the circuitry of the PCB*

IP—*Intellectual Property.*

IPC – *Institute for Printed Circuits. An organization that publishes widely accepted standards for the electronics manufacturing industry.*

ISO – *International Standards Organization. This body has certification levels for companies and is often a requirement for a company's suppliers. ISO is typically followed by a number, which designates the type of certification the factory will have, including: repair, manufacturing, design, medical, or aerospace.*

IT—*Information Technology – Enterprise's department that handles all computer systems*

Kan Ban—*A fancy term for buffer stock. A designated staging area in the manufacturing process.*

JDM— *Joint Design for Manufacture. A company or service of providing design support to an OEM. See ODM, EMS.*

JIT—*Just In Time. A style of manufacturing that limits on hand inventory and times the receipt of materials closely to when they are needed in the manufacturing process.*

Lean – *A style of manufacturing that streamlines everything and pushes liability and risk further down in the "value chain".*

LOC – *Letter of Credit. A financial arrangement where funds are escrowed for payment of goods, should agreed terms not be met.*

Mil—*Abbreviation for military.*

MIN- *Minimum (order Qty). The minimum amount that must be purchased for each purchase order. Typically dictated by the packaging of the components to be purchased.*

MOQ- *Minimum Order Quantity. MIN*

MRB-*Material Review Board. A committee that dispositions defective items reported on a DMR.*

MRP—*Material Requirements Planning. A system or software application that aids the scheduling of manufacturing by calculating and managing parts availability. See ERP.*

MULT – *The amounts of a component that must be purchased in blocks, after the minimum is met. Typically dictated by the packaging of the components.*

NPI -*New Product Introduction*

NRE—*Non-recurring Engineering. Typically a charge, or effort to prepare to manufacture a product.*

ODM—*Original Design for Manufacture. Contract manufacturing company that provides reference designs for products or will design complete product for an OEM*

OEM—*Original Equipment Manufacturer. A product company.*

OOC- *Out of Cash- The date predicted a company will be insolvent.*

O/H – *Overhead. Fixed and variable costs that are not directly related to the manufacturing of a product.*

P&L -*Profit and Loss Statement. A standardized report of financial performance for a given period of time.*

Part Master – *The identifying record of an item, typically catalogued as a part number.*

PL—*Parts List. (BOM)*

Proto – *Prototype. A very early version of a product. See alpha, beta, pilot, DFM.*

Pilot – *In manufacturing, a small pre-production run of the final or semi final product.*

PCB -*Printed Circuit Board.*

PCBA- *Printed Circuit Board Assembly.*

PLM—*Product Lifecycle Management. Software to manage product development and design. See CM, BOM, DFM, NPI*

PM—*1. Program Manager*
2. Purchasing Manager

PO – *Purchase Order.*

PPV -*Purchase Price Variance. The measurement/comparison of actual prices paid for items against the standard costs established for them.*

PTH- *Pin Through Hole. The method of assembly where a component's electrical leads are fed through a hole in the PCB and soldered in place.*

QBR- *Quarterly Business Review*

Rep – *Representative. A salesperson employed by the company manufacturing products, or the person can be an independent sales rep who makes a commission on sales for several companies they work with (synonym: sales weasel.)*

Rev – *Revision. The Revision level of a specification.*

RFI—*Request for Information. Typically a request about a company's capabilities conducted prior to an RFQ or RFP.*

RFP—*Request for Pricing, Request for Proposal. Same as RFQ.*

RFQ—*Request for Quotation. A formal request that may be distributed to several suppliers for bidding (synonym: SRFQ).*

RIF- *Reduction in Force.* Lay-off.

RoHS – *Restriction of Hazardous Substance Directive. Initiated by the EC (Europe), the directive prevents certain materials to be present in items made in or imported to Europe in an effort to reduce toxic waste.*
The items restricted are: Lead, Mercury, Cadmium, Hexavalent Chromium, Polybrominated Biphenyls, and Polybrominated Diphenyl Ether. This directive is also called the lead free initiative, as it widely affected the electronics industry (solder).

SCE—*Supply Chain Execution. The process of aligning sourced materials and assemblies to be available when needed at the best prices and the best quality.*

SCES—*Supply Chain Execution System. Software designed for SCE.*

SG&A – *Sales, General and Administration. A financial data point that is typically a fixed percentage added to COGS (costs of goods sold) in a financial report.*

SMT—*Surface Mount Technology. The placing of electrical components on a solder pad rather than through a leaded hole. See PTH, PCB, PCBA.*

SOW – *Statement of Work. A document that outlines a program or project in which specific products will be developed and manufactured over time.*

SPC – *Statistical Process Control. The collecting and monitoring of data in manufacturing with respect to limits and trends that will determine an "out of control situation."*

SRFQ—*Supplier Request for Quotation. A formal request that may be distributed to several suppliers for bidding (synonym: RFQ).*

STD – *Standard. Data established for the manufacturing of a given product. Can be financial or a time increment. Actual data is then gathered and variances are reported, increasing or decreasing profits for a given time period.*

Ts&Cs—*Terms and Conditions. A company's policies regarding engaging to do business with them. Payment, Warrantee and legal action are some of the items typically covered.*

TCA / TCO – *Total Cost of Acquisition /Total Cost of Ownership. Takes into account indirect costs associated with a sourcing decision or award.*

Turns- *In manufacturing, the measurement of inventory turns or asset turns. Inventory turns is the average on hand inventory (or inventory at the close), multiplied by 12, then divided by the total cost (at Standard) of the inventory shipped for a given time period. Asset Turns take into account the Total assets of the firm and divides that by revenue for the given period.*

Turnkey- *In manufacturing, the style of outsourcing where the supplier purchases and manages the materials that are needed to the product ordered.*

UL – *Underwriters Laboratory. A certification of safety for the design and manufacturing of a product.*

WIP -*Work In Progress. Products released to manufacturing that are not completed or shipped.*

About the Author

Walt Grischuk graduated with degrees in Political Science and Economics from Boston College and became a carpenter. After a few years, the notion that "necktie = professional" won out, and in 1982 he landed in Purchasing at United Technologies.

As the electronics manufacturing industry jumped into high gear, Walt arrived at SCI in 1990, then the world's largest EMS company at a mere $1.5 Billion in revenue. Walt's roles in several CM's have included Program Management, Sales, Business Development, Executive Management, plus his own Manufacturer's Rep firm.

In 2002, he co-founded Ora Technology, a software and consultancy firm specializing in front end solutions of proposal management, data management, spend reduction, and new product introduction for manufacturing companies.

When he is not listening to Ora's clients, Walt can be found camping on Cape Cod or in Maine. When the weather turns, he, his wife, and two children retreat to their home near Boston.

Made in the USA
Middletown, DE
05 November 2015